THE BILINGUAL SCHOOL

This is a volume in the
Arno Press collection

BILINGUAL-BICULTURAL EDUCATION
IN THE UNITED STATES

See last pages of this volume
for a complete list of titles.

THE
BILINGUAL SCHOOL

A STUDY OF BILINGUALISM IN SOUTH AFRICA

E. G. MALHERBE

ARNO PRESS
A New York Times Company
New York • 1978

Editorial Supervision LUCILLE MAIORCA

———◆———

Reprint Edition 1978 by Arno Press Inc.
Reprinted by permission of Longman Group Limited

Reprinted from a copy in the Yale University Library

BILINGUAL-BICULTURAL EDUCATION IN THE UNITED STATES
ISBN for complete set: 0-405-11071-5
See last pages of this volume for titles.

Manufactured in the United States of America

———◆———

Library of Congress Cataloging in Publication Data

Malherbe, Ernst Gideon, 1895-
    The bilingual school.

    (Bilingual-bicultural education in the United States)
    Reprint of the 1946 ed. published by Longmans,
Green, London, New York.
    1. Education, Bilingual--Africa, South. I. Title.
II. Series.
LC3738.S6M3 1978   371.9'7   77-90547
ISBN 0-405-11086-3

THE
BILINGUAL SCHOOL

A STUDY OF BILINGUALISM IN SOUTH AFRICA

by

E. G. MALHERBE

*Director of Census and Statistics for the Union
of South Africa*

Introduction by

PROFESSOR T. J. HAARHOFF

University of the Witwatersrand, Johannesburg

LONGMANS, GREEN AND CO.

LONDON   ⋄   NEW YORK   ⋄   TORONTO

LONGMANS, GREEN AND CO. LTD.
OF PATERNOSTER ROW

43 ALBERT DRIVE, LONDON, S.W.19
NICOL ROAD, BOMBAY
17 CHITTARANJAN AVENUE, CALCUTTA
36A MOUNT ROAD, MADRAS

LONGMANS, GREEN AND CO.
55 FIFTH AVENUE, NEW YORK 3

LONGMANS, GREEN AND CO.
215 VICTORIA STREET, TORONTO 1

First published in Great Britain in 1946

CODE NUMBER: 98745

PRINTED IN GREAT BRITAIN
BY WESTERN PRINTING SERVICES, LTD. BRISTOL

PREFACE

THE main purpose of this study is to make available in popular form some of the results of recent researches conducted into the problems of bilingualism in so far as they are related to the controversy of the bilingual school in South Africa. These researches are part of a Bilingualism Survey conducted in 1938, which involved *inter alia* the testing of over 18,000 pupils in representative South African schools. It is the most comprehensive piece of research of its kind ever conducted on bilingualism in South Africa or in other countries. In presenting the results here only some of the main findings are given, and, owing to its popular and abbreviated form, much explanatory evidence of a statistical nature, which would have been essential in a strictly scientific publication, had of necessity to be omitted. It is hoped to remedy this shortcoming later when a full report of the Bilingualism Survey is published.

The fact, moreover, that hardly any reference is made to South African and overseas writers on this subject must not be construed as meaning that their works have been ignored. The contrary is indeed the case. They were closely studied and I learned much from them. Owing, however, to the limitations of space, I decided simply to present my survey findings as straightforwardly and concisely as possible without bolstering them up by numerous quotations from other writers. The presentation of the facts was made as objectively as possible, and the implications of these findings were only incidentally touched upon. Volumes could indeed be written on them.

In Chapter X, however, I ventured to give my own views as to the role of the school in relation to language and citizenship in South Africa. These opinions, even though they are the result of years of experience with education in South Africa and overseas, are to a certain extent subjective and are furthermore dependent upon certain fundamental assumptions regarding the nature of South Africa's political and social future. People will therefore agree or disagree with these views according as they accept or reject those fundamental assumptions as premises. The facts, however, are simply facts and must be accepted as such until the opposite is proved.

In the text (Chapter III), I have expressed my acknowledgments to my colleagues who assisted me on the Survey. To the hundreds of teachers who gave up their classes, sometimes for days, while the tests were being conducted, and who patiently filled in elaborate questionnaires regarding their schools, I owe much gratitude. To the various education departments, whose official sanction greatly facilitated the survey, I am also much indebted.

iii

Professor T. J. Haarhoff has kindly honoured this book with an introduction. From many points of view he is singularly competent to sponsor this publication. Not only has he achieved a high degree of scholarship in the field of classical literature and therefore got his roots deep down in the cultures of our western civilization, but he has done a great deal to promote language study in South Africa, particularly in Afrikaans. He has also done more than any other South African to interpret Afrikaans to the English-speaking world overseas, and he has himself enriched Afrikaans literature with writings of no mean merit. Being in close touch with the school situation as a long-standing member of the Joint Matriculation Board, he has specially interested himself in recent years in the question of the medium of instruction to be used in the public schools and has in consequence become an ardent protagonist of the bilingual school. In such an institution he sees the only sure means of achieving integration of the two sections of the community and of building a united, South African-conscious people.

E. G. MALHERBE

PRETORIA
6th September, 1943

CONTENTS

INTRODUCTION

ARE WE IN EARNEST?

It must be clearly understood that the movement for the establishment of bilingual schools, that is schools in which both official languages are used as media of instruction, has in origin and essence nothing whatever to do with party politics. Events have inevitably dragged it into the arena of party strife; but it remains a social and educational question that is "national" in the widest sense of the word. It should therefore be discussed without the distortion that belongs to party politics. All who wish to see our children better acquainted with each other and with each other's language should support the movement, whatever their party allegiance may be.

In the last resort the issue depends on the parents. The law for the Cape Province reads: "*The medium of instruction of every pupil in all the standards of any public school, up to and including the sixth standard, shall be the home language of the pupil*" (that is, as the regulations explain, "the language best known and understood by the pupil"): "*provided that the parent of any pupil shall have the right to claim that the other language shall be gradually introduced and thereafter regularly used as a second medium of instruction in accordance with the intelligence of the pupil, and in such case provision shall be made for the instruction of such pupil accordingly.*" Similar laws exist in the Transvaal and in the Orange Free State. Natal, by the Ordinance approved 7th July 1942, has accepted the dual-medium principle.

If, therefore, the parents who desire dual medium instruction were to unite and demand their rights, the Departments would have to make the necessary arrangements. We suggest that parents should form local groups, perhaps in association with *Die Afrikaanse Genootskap* or the newly founded Bilingual School Association of Johannesburg, in order to study this most important question and to mobilize public opinion in its favour.

The real question is whether we want a Union of South Africa.

For we live in a Union that is not a Union and under a bilingual system that is not bilingual. Yet if the two main white races are to continue side by side in South Africa, it is imperative that we should create unity (which is different from uniformity) and that we should be able to communicate with each other without strain; and that is only possible if we speak each other's languages. Only then shall we be perfectly at home with each other. Historically and psychologically language is of primary importance in South Africa. It has gathered round it a whole complex of emotions; it has come to be a symbol of goodwill.

1

Dr. Ernest Barker has written: "Language is not mere words. Each word is charged with associations that touch feelings and evoke thoughts. You cannot share these feelings and thoughts unless you can unlock their associations by having the key of language. You cannot enter the heart and know the mind of a nation unless you know its speech. Conversely, once you have learned that speech, you find that with it and by it you imbibe a deep and pervasive spiritual force." (*National Character*, p. 13.)

There are various grades of bilingualism from the ability merely to understand the second language in its written or spoken form to perfect proficiency in the use of both languages. Perfect bilingualism is doubtless very rare, because perfection even in one language is hardly attainable. The adult often is so busy or so placed that it is very hard for him to learn the second language. But let us at any rate save the children from isolationism: *they* do not share the handicaps of the adult if they are brought into the proper environment; and for them there should be two great aims: (1) to get to know the children who speak the other language, and (2) (largely as a result of this) to get to know the other language; no single factor is more likely to make both groups look on South Africa as their home. As far as citizenship is concerned, this is an urgent need; for daily, under our present system, our children are drifting apart, and ignorance breeds hatred—"Onbekend maak onbemind." Sir Abe Bailey saw the urgency of the problem when he made provision for a fund to enable South Africans to become really bilingual.

It seems a common-sense sort of conclusion that our children should grow up with this double knowledge. How is it that we have strayed so far from common sense?

THE BURDEN OF OUR HISTORY

The answer to this question takes us into the unhappy past. The facts of this past must be faced without fear and without favour. In 1822 Lord Charles Somerset issued his proclamation that English was to be the only official language, although the Dutch colonists outnumbered the English by eight to one. In order to apply this to the schools, English, and especially Scotch, teachers were imported. (It was said later of a certain Scotch Director of Education that if he had not quite killed education, he had certainly scotched it!)

In thus suppressing a language, Sir Charles had the example of the Dutch East India Company, which undoubtedly meant to suppress the language of the Huguenots; but here we have to remember that the Huguenots were only about two hundred in all, that they came out under contract, and that their language was not the language of the country. Still, it was considered a politic thing to suppress a language. In this respect modern administrators lagged behind the Romans, in whose long record of contact with other races there is no instance of language suppression and whose schools fostered a bilingual tradition, just as modern educationists of the twentieth century, who opposed the recognition of Afrikaans, lagged behind the Romans in their theory of language and its growth.[1]

THE ATTITUDE OF THE REPUBLICS

Broadly speaking, it may be said that up to 1914 the Afrikaner was liberal in attitude to English. Not only was he anxious to learn English, but his laws affecting the language of the English-speaking minority were eminently fair. Thus even under the Kruger regime provision was made for the learning of English after Standard II in Government schools, and a subsidy was given to English private schools if they taught the Dutch language and South African history. In the Free State under the law of 1891 English or Dutch could be used as medium up to Standard II; thereafter both languages could be used, but at least half of the subjects must be taught through the medium of Dutch. At the Cape the prevailing medium was English; but it is fair to remember that many Afrikaners, unenlightened by the educational authorities, held the view that the child was sent to school only to learn the other language; his own language "came of its own accord." Nevertheless, there were instances where the dual-medium method was employed and teachers were encouraged in the Cape Department under Sir Frederick de Waal to use it wherever possible.

This tradition has survived in the Coloured schools at the Cape, where it is often used so effectively that the Coloured children attain a higher degree of bilingualism than many European children. In this connection Major L. Marquard recounts an illuminating incident. He tells of the progress of Afrikaans in the army and of the enthusiasm of the men for bilingualism. "But," he says, "in all the hundreds of lectures I gave to the men under the Army Education Scheme, I only once had an audience that was 100 per cent bilingual. It consisted of non-commissioned officers of the Cape Coloured Corps."

We should also remember that the medium of Dutch was fast becoming artificial, even to the Afrikaans child, though it was not until 1925 that Afrikaans was generally introduced into the schools, and that the Afrikaans language had not yet had a chance to show its capabilities. Hence it is dangerous to import our present outlook into Republican times, as many writers do, just as it is fallacious to adduce arguments from unilingual countries or from countries like Wales or Belgium and Canada, where the problem is utterly different because the languages are generally territorially separate and the proportion of bilingual people far smaller. And the evidence of German professors who have never

[1] See Horace, *Ars Poetica*, 46–7, which contains interesting parallels for the development of Afrikaans (*Die Skrywerskring Jaarboek*, 1912). For bilingualism in ancient Rome, see Haarhoff: *The Stranger at the Gate*, pp. 162 ff., 309 ff.

lived in South Africa (quoted in the minority report of the Transvaal Education Commission) cannot help us.

THE LAWS OF SMUTS AND HERTZOG

In the period between the end of the South African War and the Union the prevailing policy of the then fashionable Imperialism was to anglicize the Afrikaner through the schools. But just before Union the Smuts law in the Transvaal (1907) and the Hertzog law in the Free State (1908) pointed to a truer conception of South Africa's destiny. Under the former, instruction was given in Dutch and two other subjects were taught through the medium of Dutch if so desired; under the latter, both languages were compulsory for all after Standard II, with exemptions under certain conditions. Those who criticize the Smuts law for making the second language optional should remember that there was a larger unassimilated English element in the Transvaal than in the Free State. The important part of the Hertzog law was the provision that after Standard IV[1] up to Matriculation English and Dutch should "as far as practicable be used as the medium of instruction to an equal extent." This is an unequivocal acceptance of the dual-medium principle. But what do we mean by the dual medium?

SEPARATE, PARALLEL AND DUAL SYSTEMS

In a country like ours there are roughly three ways of dealing with bilingualism in the secondary school.

(1) We may have separate schools in which the second language is used in the school only when it is taught as a subject.
(2) We may group the children in separate classrooms but in the same school, instructing each group through the medium of its own language. This is the "parallel medium" system. Its disadvantage is that it may emphasize the idea of separateness by putting children into separate classrooms, with the result that they tend to remain socially separate and entertain exaggerated ideas of the difference between the groups. Much, however, depends on the principal and the tone of the school. Tests have shown that the mere fact of having the two sections in the same school eliminates, under the right principal, much of the bitterness found in many single-medium schools. This system is sometimes combined with the third method, the dual-medium method, described below.
(3) We may have both sections in the same classroom, and make them all do part of their work in the one language and part in the other. This is the dual-medium system, which may be applied in various

[1] Non-South African readers may like to know that the average age of children in Standard I is approximately 8 years, while that of Standard IV is about 11 years with an increase of one year per Standard up to Standard X.

ways. For example, the subject may be taken throughout in the same language, or the teacher may give translations or summaries in the other language as he goes along in each subject. This dual-medium system has the advantage of bringing the pupils together and making them feel that they are all doing the same work and doing it in both languages. It has the further advantage of making the pupil use the second language as a medium; and we have ample evidence that the present weakness of the second language is largely due to the fact that it is not used as an instrument. Experience has shown that the right stage for the introduction of this method is in most cases after Standard IV.

The third system is therefore the right one for those who are honest about Article 137 of the Union Constitution; it is a test of sincerity for those who talk about co-operation.

PREVAILING POST-UNION OPINION IN FAVOUR OF DUAL MEDIUM

General Hertzog's law was reaffirmed by Dr. W. J. Viljoen as Director of Education in the Free State in 1910; its principles, indeed, had been the tradition of the Free State from the days of Dr. Brebner. The 1910 law envisaged (a) mother-tongue medium up to Standard IV, and (b) after Standard IV three main subjects in one language and three in the other. Similarly a Select Committee of Parliament in 1910, reviewing education in South Africa as a whole, recommended mother-tongue medium up to Standard IV, and thereafter free choice to parents as to the medium. Where however such choice was not exercised, the recommendation was that "as far as practicable the second language shall be taught as a subject *and used as a medium*."

It may be said, therefore, that at this time the consensus of opinion was that in the later stages of school education both languages should be used as media. In the country schools it was a common practice; and we have seen that it is used in many Coloured schools at the Cape to-day. Why then did we depart from this sane outlook? Why has the air become thick with emotionalized educational theories in favour of separate schools? Why are politicians so vehement about the question?

ORIGIN OF SEPARATE SCHOOLS

At this point the unhappy past again obtrudes itself. It is broadly a fact that the bulk of the English-speaking population, influenced by the old Imperialism, rejected the dual-medium system: that is they rejected the ideal of a fully bilingual education. For let us have no illusions: we are not producing bilingual schoolchildren and we never shall, as long as the second language is not used as an instrument of expression and not merely as a subject to be learned for an examination. In other words, the second language must be used as a medium in the school.

The result of this opposition was that the pendulum swung in the direction of separate Government schools, and to-day they are becoming more and more separate. Politicians exploit the position by trying to capture the school for their party in ways not always apparent to the casual observer. But in trying to understand why the pendulum has swung so violently towards single-medium schools we must be fair to the Afrikaner.

WHAT THE AFRIKANER HAS ACHIEVED

We must remember his long struggle for the recognition of Afrikaans —his fight against political opposition and pedantic obtuseness. He was opposed not only by the educational authorities of English origin but also by those who came from Holland. Between Scylla and Charybdis he steered a perilous course and won home with difficulty. He gained a point that now seems obvious and that is illustrated by the history of the Romance languages and of English itself. But the fight was bitter when Church elders could oppose Afrikaans by saying: "Why, even Moses wrote High Dutch!"

Hence he regards his language as a precious possession and is extremely jealous of anything that seems to threaten it. At the same time he has developed since 1900 a literature of great freshness and vigour, holding a promise of great things if it is not starved by isolationism, a literature that is rooted in the soil and is rightly regarded by him as peculiarly his own. Even where there are weak spots (and there are many) he is inclined to say with Touchstone: "An ill-favoured thing, sir, but mine own." He is, therefore, anxious to safeguard the young and tender plant and to prevent it from getting lost in the huge forest of English literature; so he builds a wall around it.

And it must be said that in the school and elsewhere he has done much to weed his garden. The barbarisms of an earlier generation such as "ek het my ge-enjoy" are no longer found in decent circles. The language has attained a new purity and vigour. English-speaking people should try to appreciate the adventure of discovering new and expressive turns of speech and making experiments in new fields. The part played by the school in creating this new pride in language and in discovering technical terms (already existing in Nederlands) is important and deserving of our appreciation.

Progress has been rapid and the Afrikaner who has emerged from his former state of uninspiring hybridism is apt to be impatient with Afrikaners who are still in that state or with English-speaking people who do not appreciate his experience. He looks to the Afrikaans-medium school to maintain the purity of his language and the individuality of his character. He wants his children to have the same pride in the progress of the Afrikaner as he has.

ISOLATIONISM NO SAFEGUARD

All this we must understand and appreciate. But isolation will not preserve, it will only impoverish this cultural advance. Instead of building a wall round it, the Afrikaner should share it with his English-speaking citizens, and by so doing he will find himself enriched; it will be like the parable of the loaves and fishes. Crude arithmetic makes Afrikaners think that when you advocate a 50/50 language policy for the post-primary school you impoverish the Afrikaans' inheritance. In reality, as Dr. Malherbe's investigation has shown, the home language, so far from losing, actually gains in the bilingual school, having been securely established in the earlier stages. On the other hand more thorough knowledge of the other language enriches the mind of the pupil without destroying the individuality of his home-language tradition.

NOT FUSION BUT CO-OPERATION

For we must frankly face the fact that we cannot talk glibly of fusion. The Afrikaner who is anxiously guarding his cultural advance will run a mile from fusion, fearing just that relapse into what he describes as soulless imitation from which he set forth to find his soul.

We should, at the present time, aim at co-operation, respecting the individuality of both traditions. That is healthy nationalism which is not incompatible with internationalism. We should create in the school an atmosphere in which the two traditions are looked on not as hostile and incompatible, but as complementary to one another in South African education. We must teach our children, not that there is a section which will ultimately dominate and produce a unilingual state, but that, just as Rome produced the best citizens when its two languages (Greek which originally came from over the sea, and Latin, the language of the Roman farmer) had learned to co-operate, so the "complete" South African is the man who is at home in both languages —*homo utriusque linguae*—who has made two cultural traditions his own. Our children are eager to embark on this great adventure if only we give them the proper guidance.

To-day, unfortunately, owing largely to political circumstances, many Afrikaners are dissuading our children from this creative task and implanting ideas of separateness and incompatibility. To our plea that the proverb "Onbekend maak onbemind" (*Unknown makes unloved*) suggests free association of the two sections in the same school, they reply with an English proverb: "Familiarity breeds contempt." This argument was actually circulated to heads of schools by a certain sectional organization that is trying to keep the races apart. It is fantastic nonsense.

REAL CO-OPERATION

What actually happens when the children of the two sections associate freely together, uninfluenced by the twisted nationalism that has been the curse of the modern world, is that they find no difficulty in making friends. How often have we seen people who are full of abstract hatred for the other race betray their theory and reveal their own innate friendliness, when they get to know the person they are supposed to hate? Give children work to do together or interests to develop in common, as is done in the dual-medium school, and race hatred disappears.

Nor should our Afrikaner friends forget that General Hertzog, the founder of the Afrikaner Nationalism, is also one of the founders of the dual-medium system. Hence it is the more to be regretted that the former followers of General Hertzog, who understood the meaning of co-operation better than any, should now be opposing the bilingual school. Formerly the objectors to the bilingual principle were mainly English; to-day they are to a large extent Afrikaners. And now the English and the Afrikaner extremists agree with one another. Both want unilingualism. But as each wants it for his own language they are not likely to agree for long; and between them they do educational injury to the large body of children whose home language is not exclusively either English or Afrikaans but both. (In Dr. Malherbe's tests these form something like 43 per cent of the whole.)

What is it that they are saying? Some of them remind one of the Scotsman who had been made an elder of the Church and to whom a candid friend once said: "What qualification have you for this responsible position? You can't speak, you can't argue, you've done nothing for the cause." To whom the proud elder replied: "Ay, mon, but ye ken I'm a grand objector."

THE MOTHER TONGUE

One of the things the objectors are saying against the bilingual school is that it is a violation of the mother-tongue principle. It is not. There is general agreement all over the educational world that the child should begin his education in his mother tongue or, as the Hertzog law put it, the language he most easily understands. For this the foundation is laid in the earlier part of the primary school, after which the second language is introduced as a *subject* and could be used in some cases as a *medium* even in the primary schools. That is the first part of our programme—the primary school, with the mother tongue predominating as a medium of instruction.

CONTACT BETWEEN THE TWO GROUPS

But in order that the children shall meet each other, we should like to see English and Afrikaans-speaking children brought together in the same *primary* school on the "parallel" system. It may even be possible in some cases (it has been done) to run a parallel system in the same classroom, repeating the instruction in the other language so that each group hears its own medium and yet has the advantage of picking up the other language.

Now it is a sad reflection on our classroom methods of teaching that children learn a language more easily from one another than from a formal teacher. This has been shown over and over again in our country: get children to play together, interested in doing something together, and they astonish you by the speed with which, by trial and error, they acquire each other's language.

Here we have an important fact that should be used; and one of the most fruitful ways of using it is to exchange children during the vacations. In a scheme worked out by Mr. J. W. du Preez, of King Edward's School, Johannesburg, town children were sent to selected homes on the platteland, where they made friends with Afrikaner children and learned their language. It is this system that we want, not the practice of sending town children *en bloc* to farm-schools to associate with themselves. It is a scheme that should be organized on a Union-wide scale. If properly run, it could change a negative and sectional outlook into a positive and creative one in a single generation. That is the second stage of our proposal.

If this were done towards the end of the primary school period children should be fully prepared to take some of their high school subjects in the second language. "Yes, but they will fight," says the grand objector. Not with proper control; but even if they do, it is better for them to have it out at this stage than to grow up cherishing hatred and suspicion in their hearts. A physical fight may even act as a *katharsis* and lead to mutual respect afterwards.

OTHER OBJECTIONS

The objectors who signed Minority Report No. 13 of the Transvaal Education Commission (1937) had a large number of criticisms. One of the more important was that religious teaching in the separate school is simpler because you can teach the child the same form of religion that he is used to in the home. We should reply that school religious teaching should concentrate mainly on the historical aspect of the Bible, but that if more than this is required, it could quite well be arranged for ministers to visit the children of their denomination. The purely theological aspect of religion is the business of the Church and its absence in the school need not mean the absence of a Christian spirit. The New Testament clearly indicates love of one's neighbour as one of the two pillars of the Christian faith. It is only too clear, as Dr. Malherbe's tests have shown, that the separate system, with its isolationism, often fosters hatred of one's neighbour under the guise of patriotic duty. This hatred is not inborn; it is largely created by the circumstances of the separate school. In practice it generally disappears, as we have seen, when the children get to know each other and come to do things together. That has also been the experience of the army.

Another objection was that national sentiment connected with Kruger Day and Dingaan's Day would be hampered if the two sections were present in the same school. We reply that any sentiment which is sound and constructive in the building of a South African nation (and we include the sentiment connected with the festivals mentioned) can and should be fully expounded in any school; any sentiment which cannot be fully expounded has no right to be taught at all. It is precisely in the school that children should learn to appreciate the good things on both sides, admit the wrong things done by their own side, and admire what was well done by the other. Anything else is dishonest citizenship and perverted nationalism. And here it may be noted, as a sign of growing South Africanism, that there has lately been a movement on the part of English-speaking citizens to join in the celebration of Dingaan's Day. Our effort should be to foster joint festivals.

The objectors also stated that "the desired co-operation between the two groups in this country is coming in a natural way and is improving from year to year." This was before the war. Perhaps now they will think differently; for there is abundant evidence to the contrary.

Then there is the objector who talks about intelligence quotients. To him Dr. Malherbe's figures should bring enlightenment; it may be stated that even in the primary school Coloured children at the Cape and Indian children in Natal frequently manage quite well with a dual-medium system, and there is an experiment going on at present with subnormal children in Johannesburg which promises good results.

POLITICAL ARGUMENT

But the most insistent objector approaches the problem from the political angle. The result of the bilingual system will be a miserable mongrel, neither one thing nor the other, "nasionaal ontaard." Much nonsense has been talked about the "foreign" medium warping the soul of the child and doing it an irreparable injury. There are plenty of instances in South Africa of men whose souls are still genuinely Afrikaans and "nasionaal" in spite of their training in "the other language." It all depends how and at what stage you are introduced to the other medium; we make bold to say that in the system we advocate no soul-distortion will take place. Nor can anyone maintain that the pupils of the Stellenbosch Boys' High School, under Mr. Paul Roos, or of the Bethal High School, under Mr. P. I. Hoogenhout,[1] emerged as miserable mongrels, "nasionaal ontaard." Indeed, the opposite is the case. But a certain type of mind, influenced sometimes by the Nazi creed, thinks of a 100 per cent insistence on one's own language as the course of the strong man. Actually it is the weak man who cannot afford to be tolerant and many-sided.

THE HISTORICAL TRADITION

Some have maintained: "Dual-medium education directly conflicts with our national tradition and the history of our schools"; and in an article by "an authoritative educationist" in *Die Huisgenoot* (14th May 1943) the dual medium is called a "brand new idea." But historically the dual medium is the system of the Boer Republics and to a large extent of the Cape. What is new is not the dual-medium system but the frenzied protests against it; it is *they* that are contrary to our Afrikaans tradition.

Others have said: "In a mixed company the Afrikaner will always speak English because of his natural politeness." The answer seems to be: the sooner we have dual-medium education the better; then there will be no need for the Afrikaner to overdo either his English or his politeness.

THE PRIVATE SCHOOL

Then there is the old accusation that the existence of English private schools shows that the English-speaking section is not in earnest about bilingualism. There are historical reasons for the founding of the private schools and they have shown a steady advance in South Africanism. For example, whereas some years ago many boys at St. John's College, Johannesburg, took French for matriculation, to-day almost 100 per cent take Afrikaans and the school is keen on raising the standard of its Afrikaans. Another private High School for Boys is reported to be contemplating the introduction of the dual-medium system. As I write I have before me a letter from a headmistress of a large private school asking for help in appointing a mistress to teach geography in Afrikaans throughout the school.

But the private schools form a small minority. It is from the body of parents whose children go to Government schools that the demand for dual-medium instruction is coming; and that those who make the demand are largely English-speaking is shown by the voluntary adoption

[1] Mr. Hoogenhout adopted the following procedure in 1910 under the directorship of Mr. (now Sir John) Adamson. After Standard IV the second language was gradually introduced as medium, with the result that when the children entered the Secondary School they were able "without exception to take any subject in either language." Approximately half of the subjects were taught in English and half in Afrikaans. "The majority of the pupils were quite definitely more bilingual than children who to-day attend a single-medium High School." There was a fine spirit of co-operation and no racialism.

B

of the system in some Pretoria and Johannesburg schools and by the formation in Johannesburg of a Bilingual School Association.

"Love for your own language," said a University rector, "is incompatible with love for another language." This is surely just as fatuous as the argument that because an abstraction called perfect bilingualism is unattainable the bilingual school is a waste of time. Love for South Africa *should* include love for both official languages, as well as for the Bantu languages, and *may* include a number of other languages, both ancient and modern. The capacity for appreciation depends on the bigness of the person.

But again and again we find that the Afrikaner is obsessed by that old bogy, fear of absorption. This is historically understandable, and colour is lent to it by certain voices that still make themselves heard in the Press. It is incumbent on our English-speaking citizens to dispel this fear and by their deeds to assure the Afrikaner of his cultural security. On the other hand the Afrikaner should remember that at least some of the aggressiveness of his leaders on this question is due to the fact that isolationism in school and society has produced ignorance of the second language and hence a feeling of inferiority. To compensate for this they have evolved the doctrine (new to the Afrikaner) that unilingualism is a virtue. This they attempt to justify by false arguments drawn from unilingual countries and by the false notion that bilingual secondary education will detract from the Afrikaner's ability to speak his own language. The truth is that the bilingual child is a more intelligent pupil and makes a better educated man and a better citizen of South Africa.

CONTAMINATION

Another objector thinks that the well of English, pure and undefiled, will be contaminated if the languages are in juxtaposition and that the issue will be some sort of "Anglikaans." What this objector often means is that English accent and idiom are affected by "South African" English. Barbarous mixtures on the Afrikaans side have been largely banished by the new pride the Afrikaner has learned to take in his language. A certain amount of mutual influence there is bound to be; but once a sound foundation has been laid in the mother tongue there is little serious danger. Our experience has shown that it is possible for two languages and two cultures to live side by side and enrich each other without losing their character. For an additional language is an enrichment; *zovele talen ik kan, zovele malen ben ik 'n man*: and English South Africans are beginning to see that on the intellectual side Afrikaans is a key to Dutch, German, Old English and other Germanic languages, while on the aesthetic side it is a passport to an interesting literature and provides for citizenship an intimate insight into an element that forms 60 per cent of the white population.

AN AWAKENING

English-speaking South Africa is waking up to the importance of bilingualism. The attitude of many Afrikaners on this point, as they recall the past, may be summed up in the ironical question: "How can we believe it?" But believe it or not, it requires no Ripley to demonstrate this new attitude on the part of very many English-speaking South Africans. This is to some extent connected with the change in England, where the old Imperialism is fading into the background. I have received scores of letters on the subject, and it is not too much to say that public opinion is moving ahead of the authorities. In the Army, too, where our lads face a common danger, there has been much progress in bilingualism and in true South Africanism; the late General Dan Pienaar's influence on his men is one of the proofs of this.

It is right that at this stage the move should come from the English section, and it is more than gratifying that the province of Natal should have been the first in the most recent period of our education to make a large-scale experiment in the dual medium. We need more experiments, for the subject bristles with practical difficulties. We need private schools, for they are freer to experiment than provincial departments, and we need enlightened public opinion to reverse the present trend of educational policy. According to the *Bulletin of Educational Statistics* (1940), the percentage of pupils in secondary classes in the Transvaal who receive instruction in both media in more or less equal proportions, decreased from 10·5 in 1932 to 1·6 in 1939, and in the Union from 20·6 to 9·3. We are moving fast in the direction of separateness, which brings with it ignorance of other people and their language, fostering in consequence suspicion and strife.

LOW STANDARD OF THE SECOND LANGUAGE

There is the further point that the second language is in a parlous state. Anybody who doubts this statement should read the Government Report on the position of the languages in our eduational system (1941). The Commission puts its finger on the weak spot when it points out that the second language is "learned up" as a subject and is not used as an instrument of expression, implying that it should be used as a medium in order to be learned effectively.

GENERAL REFORM

Nobody expects a change overnight. Some schools have already begun by teaching one subject in the second language, and from this they progress to two or three subjects according to their circumstances. The process of readjustment will have to be gradual and for some time there may not be much response from the Afrikaans side. But once the right course is set, the goal will come into view; and the stars that must guide our course are, first, progressively more contact between the children of the two white races, a contact that will be deliberately fostered by our educational system instead of being, as now, discouraged; and, secondly, a progressively greater bilingualism, promoted and strengthened by a system such as we have described.

NORMAL COLLEGES

One of the most needed reforms is the reorganization of the Teachers' Training Colleges. To-day an all but unilingual teacher is turned out by an all but unilingual Normal College, and he goes back to his unilingual village to teach the other language in one of those small schools that carry most of the education on the platteland. It is a vicious circle. Soon (like the emperors in the 4th century A.D.) we shall be unable to find really bilingual teachers. The reform is most urgent. What we want is the application of the dual-medium principle to *all* training colleges.

SAVE THE CHILDREN

A girl who passed her matriculation in an Afrikaans-medium school in the northern Transvaal told me that, even working as she did in an Afrikaans firm in Johannesburg, she bitterly regretted her weakness in the other language. She, like many others, felt herself economically and socially handicapped.

A lad came to me not long ago. He had been to a large English-medium school in Johannesburg. He had emerged with a matriculation certificate in Afrikaans, but unable to speak the language. He had emerged, moreover, full of cheap generalizations about Afrikaners and a distaste for them based on ignorance. Then he went to Onderstepoort, where his ignorance of Afrikaans and Afrikaners was amended, for the system was bilingual in our sense of the term. He became at last a South African in the full sense, greatly to his own joy. A new South African had been created. English and Afrikaner lads all over the Union are being kept from realizing that it is our task to create a Union, and in most cases without the saving grace of Onderstepoort.

There is increasing ignorance of the second language; ignorance brings a feeling of inferiority, and that in turn brings aggressive assertion that it is a good thing to be unilingual and that strength lies in isolationism. Let us save our children from isolationism. The adult, with all the worries of a busy life and the handicap of an unfavourable environment, finds it difficult to acquire a new language and to break down group barriers; to a child it is "child's play." The world is moving away from the isolationist principle. Even America could not maintain it. More and more, in politics, in economics, in education, the realization must dawn that the world is one in the sense that no part can be completely isolated from the rest. Fullness of life, educationally and spiritually, is not compatible with the barbed-wire fences of racial politics. With the sun of a new world rising over the grandeur of our limitless veld, the darkness of estranging barriers will yield; it will yield before the creative inspiration of giving ourselves to South Africa—ourselves undivided to her undivided:

Ons vir jou, Suid-Afrika!

. . . .

There is no need to praise the scientific investigation undertaken by Dr. E. G. Malherbe: it will remain a monument in the educational history not only of South Africa but of the world; a work by a scholar who exemplifies in himself the qualities of South Africanism that he tries to create in others.

T. J. HAARHOFF

CHAPTER I

BILINGUALISM IN SOUTH AFRICA:
WHAT DO WE MEAN BY IT?

IN this discussion I am confining myself to the phenomenon of bilingualism *as it is found in South Africa*. The two languages dealt with are the two official languages, *English* and *Afrikaans*. The African vernaculars are not considered here. In many respects, the South African situation with regard to bilingualism is unique. The high degree of geographic and social interspersion of the two languages, and the consequent relatively high proportion of South Africans who speak both languages, make comparisons on bilingualism even with other so-called bilingual countries like Canada, Wales, Belgium, etc., not to mention the dozens of other countries where more than one language is spoken, a very risky business. For example, the percentage of South Africans who speak both official languages (English and Afrikaans) is five times as big as the percentage of Canadians who speak both official languages (English and French). According to the 1936 Union Census, 64·4 per cent of the Europeans aged 7 years and over "were able to speak" both English and Afrikaans, 19 per cent English only, 16·4 per cent Afrikaans only and 2 per cent neither. In 1918 only 42·1 per cent could speak both. The advance of bilingualism in South Africa has been considerable ever since the formation of Union in 1910. This is principally due to the statutory recognition of equal rights for Afrikaans and English as official languages embodied in the Act of Union. The *rate* of increase in bilingualism has, however, definitely been slowing down during the last ten years.

.   .   .   .

At first sight the term "bilingualism" seems plain and definite, but read the current literature in this country, talk the matter over, and a large variety of meanings and interpretations will be encountered. This range of meanings extends all the way from a colloquial knowledge of the mother tongue plus a very casual acquaintance with the other tongue (the latter perhaps being limited to an ability to swear appropriately and to say "yes" and "no" in that language) to the other end, where is supposed to be found the ideal state of perfection in both languages unattainable by any human being—a sort of Joost van den Vondel and William Shakespeare rolled into one.

It is a well-known phenomenon in scientific, and especially in philosophical, discussions, that as soon as any term or name is used to designate different concepts, confusion of thought arises. One man

17

uses the term in one sense and the other in another sense, with the result that they argue past each other and never seem to reach a common ground of understanding. And, as I shall attempt to show presently, it is this very difficulty which besets our discussions on the language question and has been responsible for much of the trouble and misunderstanding which have of late arisen in that connection. One of the commonest misapprehensions is to regard *bi*lingualism as synonymous with *equi*lingualism (see p. 26 below).

The time has come, therefore, when we should clarify our concepts on this matter, and by way of a start I am going to make an attempt at defining a few of the possible meanings of the term "bilingualism." In reality there is an infinite number. They range themselves all the way along a scale from zero to 100 per cent; but for simplicity's sake I am going to divide the whole gamut into six stages or steps which correspond roughly to certain social and professional demands. "Bilingual-for-what" is to be the criterion. When new demands arise it will of course be possible to make the gradation of steps a little finer.

In every case of bilingualism we shall take for granted that a man has a first language and a second language. Some prefer to call these his mother tongue and his other tongue respectively. By the first language, or mother tongue, we mean the language of the home, the fireside, the language in which he thinks most often, in which he expresses the "dear and intimate things"[1] and in which he has probably reached a greater all-round proficiency than in any other language. By a second language or other tongue I mean the language in which he is less generally proficient and which comes less naturally to him.

There are exceptions to this general distinction. For example, some people may in some large department of their lives (e.g. in their scientific studies) use their second language exclusively, confining the use of their mother tongue mostly to the more colloquial forms of communication outside that particular universe of discourse. What is therefore their first language in ordinary, everyday speech becomes their second language when they switch on to some subject requiring a special vocabulary.

Or again, owing to changes in his place of abode or occupation, a man may find that through disuse of what was at one time his first language (or mother tongue) and through use of the other tongue they have actually changed places. During this change a point may have been reached where the two just balanced each other before the scales swung over to the other side. This reversal may take place in the same department of life and is slightly different from the former case, which may be regarded as an exception.

But even in the latter case we may find that the mother tongue

---

[1] A phrase used by Michael West: *Bilingualism* (with special reference to Bengal), Bureau of Education, India, Occasional Reports, No. 13, 1926.

(or what was at one time the first language) may come very well to the fore in times of emotional stress. When, for instance, a man is very angry or very afraid, he may revert to the language he learnt at his mother's knee, as in Bernard Shaw's *Pygmalion*, where "Galatea" (Miss Doolittle) in a moment of great indignation breaks through the veneer of the "other" tongue and shocks her genteel environment with a "Not bloody loikely!" These are however exceptional circumstances and in what follows I shall confine myself to the general rule and not to the exceptions.

SIX STAGES OF BILINGUALISM[1]

While realizing that there are very few, if any, people who are 100 per cent proficient in their mother tongue or first language (even in the absence of another tongue or second language), and that ability in the first language may vary greatly amongst individuals according to the native capacity and the training of the particular person in question, I am going in the following steps to gauge a man's bilinguality chiefly by the extent of his general proficiency in the second language in order to meet certain practical situations in South African life.

STAGE I. At this stage a man must be able *to follow intelligently* an ordinary conversation, speech or sermon in the second language, both in its written and spoken form. He must at least be able to appreciate a joke in that language, unless it involves too many linguistic subtleties. He must, as a citizen in a bilingual country, be able at least to read the newspapers for himself in the second language as well as his own. In an exceptional case, where he finds himself alone among people who cannot understand his mother tongue at all, he will probably succeed in making himself understood at a pinch. (If he be of French or Hebrew descent, the facile use of gestures may prove to be a great asset in such a contingency!) But the ability to speak the second language with any degree of fluency is not a *sine qua non* at this stage.

The requirements of this stage represent to me the lowest possible stage to which the term bilinguality can legitimately be applied. They are however of such a nature that communication is made possible between English and Afrikaans-speaking people, whether they can speak each other's language or not.

These minimum requirements will enable each person in a company to speak the language that comes most natural to him and in which he can express himself best without fear of not being understood and, consequently, of being considered rude. No one feels "out of it" in not being able to follow everything that is going on in the conversation. Neither is anyone made to feel awkward by the fact (as so often

---

[1] These stages were outlined by the writer in evidence before the Transvaal Provincial Education Commission and were printed in Appendix I of their Report (T.P., No. 5, of 1939).

happens) that the majority of the company are speaking their second language with a good deal of unnaturalness, merely in order to be polite to him because he does not understand their first language. This happens more frequently where there is one English-speaking person present among a group of Afrikaans-speaking persons than the other way about.

When once this stage has been reached it will make unnecessary the requirement exacted of prominent citizens to-day at big public functions, when like the Governor-General or the Prime Minister they have to repeat their speeches verbatim in both languages—a practice which is not only tiring to the speakers but also boring to their hearers. They could then simply start their addresses in one language and conclude them in the other without having to repeat themselves. Thereby they would not only give due recognition to both, but also be assured that they have been understood by all their hearers.

I must repeat that the requirements at this stage constitute absolutely the minimum requirements necessary for proper citizenship in a bilingual country like South Africa, where there is such a great interspersion of the two sections. We cannot have anything less if we want to build up a common understanding between the two sections in this country. If men can understand each other's language they have already laid the foundation for a better appreciation of each other's viewpoint. This minimum must be the common possession of the masses, because then only will we have in our languages a means for the effective integration of the two sections. With anything less than this minimum the presence of two languages in a young country like this will continue to be a dividing rather than a unifying factor. As the results of our investigations will show, every step which we succeed in getting beyond this absolute minimum is a step towards achieving greater understanding, tolerance and unity between English and Afrikaans-speaking South Africans.

STAGE II. The second stage will require in addition to the above an ability to *converse intelligibly* and with a fair amount of fluency in the second language. At this stage the accent will probably not be perfect nor the idiom pure, but the person can make himself understood for all practical purposes. This level of attainment will probably suffice in most businesses where both languages are spoken, e.g. in the work of waiters, shopkeepers, salesmen, conductors, etc. The ability to write the second language is not an essential at this stage, though the ability to understand, speak and read it is essential.

Still within this stage, but perhaps bordering on the following stage, can be put the ability to read and enjoy the literature of the second language. With the ordinary man this will be chiefly the reading of easy fiction in books and magazines. Here the second language ceases to be an obstacle and begins to be an opportunity. New vistas are opened up and the life of the individual is enriched. At this stage the English-speaking South African ought to be able to read and enjoy Afrikaans magazines, like *Die Huisgenoot*, *Brandwag* or *Naweek* and ordinary fiction like Langenhoven's *Sonde met die Bure* or Sangiro's *Oerwoud en Vlakte* or *Op Safari* and, perhaps later on, Van Bruggen's "Ampie" series and the works of C. M. v.d. Heever. The Afrikaans-speaking South African ought at this stage to read and enjoy not only the current English fiction found in our libraries to-day but also Scott and Dickens and Stevenson, to mention only a few of the easier classics, which are regarded as more or less common property in the cultural background of most English-speaking people.

In this respect the Afrikaans-speaking South African stands to gain more from his second language, English, as he generally realizes, than his English-speaking friend who learns Afrikaans as a second language.[1] In saying this, I do not desire to detract in any way from the beautiful, entertaining and fast-growing literature that has been produced in the short life of Afrikaans as a written language, because there exists to-day a greater amount of worth-while reading matter in Afrikaans than even a very ambitious English-speaking South African could manage to get through. Nevertheless it cannot be denied that the English language, having become practically a world language and having developed a great literature during many hundreds of years, does open up more vistas from an aesthetic, a scientific and even a mere entertainment point of view than Afrikaans can offer to the English-speaking person at this stage.

It is true that one may gain access to the great Nederlands literature through Afrikaans, which in a way supplies this deficiency in the Afrikaans background. It would however be over-optimistic to expect many people, to whom Afrikaans is a second language, to gain access to the Nederlands literature at this stage of their linguistic development. At most such access would be limited to those who have the privilege of higher education in this language. These constitute less than one in a thousand of the population.

[1] Arsenian in his study: *Bilingualism and Mental Development*, 1937 (p. 12), puts the same idea in a more general way:

"The monoglot, especially the one from the small language group, will either share in the present civilization and therefore become a bilinguist or be deprived of the benefits of it for the sake of his monoglotism. The following quotation from H. G. Wells epitomizes the situation aptly: 'The inducements to an English-man, Frenchman or German to become bilingual are great enough nowadays, but the inducements to a speaker of the smaller languages are rapidly approaching compulsion. He must do it in self-defence. To be an educated man in his own vernacular has become an impossibility. He must either become a mental subject of one of the greater languages or sink to the intellectual status of the peasant.' " (*Anticipations of the Reaction of Mechanical and Scientific Progress upon Human Life and Thought* (London, 1902) p. 248.)

For the effects of unilingual Greek culture as compared with bilingual Roman culture on racial tolerance in the ancient world, see Haarhoff: *The Stranger at the Gate*.

STAGE III. This stage includes all the requirements of Stages I and II and in addition *the ability to write the second language correctly.* This stage constitutes in my opinion the minimum which can be expected from a clerk or secretary in an ordinary business or in the Government Service, if he wishes to be termed bilingual. That is he must be able to reply to any letter in the language in which it was written. In so doing he need not reach the height of literary excellence, but whatever he writes in the second language must be free from grammatical and spelling errors and without gross violations of idiom—in short, he must reach a level of correctness that is usually expected from any good business firm in its correspondence.

At this stage I do not regard a perfect accent as a *sine qua non.* What is wanted here is an efficient paper-language. As examples of what has been done at this stage I may quote the case of English-speaking civil servants and ministers from Scotland who took up service under the Free State and Transvaal Governments in the old Republican days. Their pronunciation was by no means perfect, as many humorous anecdotes from those days serve to illustrate, but they wrote their second language (Nederlands, which is considerably more difficult for an outsider to pick up than Afrikaans is to-day) with a precision and correctness which can very well be emulated by bilingual civil servants of to-day. Messrs. Brebner and Buchanan in the Civil Service and the Murrays and McGregors and Frasers in the church are typical examples of what I mean. There are hundreds more cases which can be quoted to show that the requirements at this stage are well within the reach of every civil servant if there is but the will to achieve them.

STAGE IV. In Stages I, II and III we have outlined the bilingual requirements for the purposes of national integration and effective citizenship, and for smaller business concerns and the higher grades of public service. We now come to the *minimum requirements of the bilingual teacher.* This stage includes the requirements mentioned in the foregoing stages and goes further. Here we want not only correctness on paper but a correct and convincing power of expression both in writing and speaking the two languages. Speech must be fluent, and both accent and idiom must be such that they can serve as fit models for growing minds to imitate. It is an excellent thing to have in every school, where possible, specialist teachers for the language instruction in the case of both the first and the second languages.

In these cases it would be eminently desirable that these specialists should have a first-language knowledge of a fairly high degree in the respective languages. Unfortunately, however, not all schools can afford special language teachers, and it is, and will remain (as far as I can see), a common thing in the majority of primary schools in this country for the class teacher to be also the language teacher of the class in both languages. In the small rural schools, which comprise over 60 per cent of the total number of European schools in South Africa, there is no alternative. This means that in these schools we simply must have competent bilingual teachers unless bilingual education is to prove a farce. Leaving the question of the medium aside for the moment, we insist that they must be able to teach both languages effectively. Unfortunately, however, we have in this class of school not only the lowest certificated teachers but also the largest number of uncertificated teachers. Owing to the fact that the rural schools are predominantly Afrikaans, it is the Afrikaans section of the community that suffers most from this deficiency in bilingual teachers. The large urban schools have specialist teachers for the two languages.

I am afraid that on the whole our system of selecting and training teachers does not recognize sufficiently the language needs of the one- and two-teacher schools, and for that matter of the majority of other primary schools. While it is true that in some institutions for training teachers special facilities have been provided for speech-training to make teachers proficient in the use of both Afrikaans and English, generally speaking the practice does not meet the country's needs. I shall give here the position in the Normal Colleges of the Transvaal, a province which has in the past always been in the forefront amongst the provinces in maintaining high standards in teacher training. I submitted all these students to a battery of standardized language tests which I had previously applied to over 18,000 schoolchildren, and for which norms for the various standards had been worked out. I give the results only for the final-year students; i.e. those who were in their third year of training after matriculation. The figures are for 1938, when this survey was made.

LANGUAGE ATTAINMENT OF ALL FINAL-YEAR STUDENTS IN TRANSVAAL NORMAL COLLEGES

Percentage Falling Below	Combined Results of the 3 Afrikaans Normal Colleges in		Results of the 1 English Normal College in	
	English Language	Afrikaans Language	English Language	Afrikaans Language
	per cent	per cent	per cent	per cent
Standard VI	6	—	—	3
,, VII	26	—	—	25
,, VIII	47	2	—	49
,, IX	65	11	2	73
,, X	77	21	5	79

From the above table it will be seen that 6 per cent of the teachers

from the Afrikaans medium Normal Colleges had not even reached the
Standard VI level in English language (i.e. the average level of English
medium children in Standard VI), 26 per cent were *below* Standard VII,
47 per cent *below* Standard VIII, and so on. The English medium
Normal College was no better in respect to Afrikaans. These figures,
which are based on tests far more objective and reliable than any of
the ordinary school examinations, deserve careful consideration.

The one outstanding fact is that about half of these students, on the
eve of their being released into the schools as teachers, had barely a
Standard VII proficiency in their second language. Incidentally, it
should be noted that even in their first language, Afrikaans, 21 per cent
of the Afrikaans Normal College students fell below the average
obtained by Afrikaans medium Standard X pupils and 5 per cent of the
English students were below Standard X average in English. The
English students seem better in their mother tongue than the Afrikaans
students. This difference is probably due to selection. It may be of
interest to note also that over 90 per cent of the Normal College students
were the products of unilingual (single medium) schools. The students
from bilingual schools did considerably better on the whole in their
second language and no worse in their first than the products of the
single medium schools.[1]

Two remedies are suggested for the situation, which is becoming
worse rather than better:

(*a*) Turn all normal and training colleges into bilingual institutions,
not only as regards medium, but also by having English and
Afrikaans-speaking student-teachers together in the same institution.

(*b*) A special bonus should be given to teachers who qualify for a
bilingual certificate.

No teacher should be given a bilingual certificate who

(1) if a *primary* teacher, is not able to (*a*) teach the second language as a
language and (*b*) use it as a medium in the other subjects;

(2) if a *secondary* teacher, cannot either teach the second language
as a subject or use it as a medium in the special subjects offered by
the teacher.

This is what our aim should be, and the requirements should be more
rigidly applied according as the facilities for carrying this consistently
into effect have been developed, e.g. in practice teaching and in speech-
training in both languages.

While teachers should be bilingual for the reasons mentioned above,
there may for the time being be quite a legitimate place for unilingual
teachers in large schools where the classes are homogeneous as regards
medium, and where they are required to teach one subject or a few

[1] See Chapter IX for the results of the Attitude Tests of these students.

subjects through one medium only. But in the case of all principals and of teachers who undertake work in the smaller schools, bilingualism, in the sense of Stage IV, ought to be a *sine qua non* of their appointment.

STAGE V. This stage is represented by the attainments of those selected few who both as users and as students of the two languages would probably reach the upper 10 percentile in both languages. Or, to put it differently, it is the stage reached by those who command a greater facility and power in the use of both languages than 90 per cent of the people who use either of these languages as their mother tongue.

The late Prof. John du Plessis, Dr. W. J. Viljoen, Senator Langenhoven, and among those living, Dr. C. L. Leipoldt, Professors J. J. Smith, M. C. Botha, Theo. Haarhoff—to mention some of my own acquaintances—are a few examples of those who have in my opinion reached this stage of bilinguality. If in the case of some of these we may look upon Afrikaans and Nederlands as one language (to distinguish it from English, which is a second language for most of them) I may venture the opinion that these men have not only reached a stage of proficiency in their mother tongue (Afrikaans) which has seldom been surpassed but have also in each case attained a level in the other tongue which is reached by relatively few English people. The remark of Schuchardt, therefore, so often quoted with approval, that "if a bilingual man has two strings to his bow, both are rather slack," is not true in all cases.[1]

Another example occurs to me as I write, viz. General Smuts. In spite of the fact that English is not his mother tongue nor his home language, it may be said without fear of contradiction that the English as used by him in his *Holism and Evolution* surpasses in power of expression and in purity of diction the English of at least 95 per cent of those who use that language as their mother tongue. The same may be said of Mr. J. H. Hofmeyr in his addresses and writings. These men,

---

[1] The often alleged inferiority of bilingual persons has been disproved by the latest psychological and educational investigations in bilingualism. Also, the study of literature shows many illustrous exceptions to Schuchardt's rather facile generalization. Cf. the observation made by Arsenian in his comprehensive study: *Bilingualism and Mental Development* (1937), p. 134:

"The indications are that, for the ages and groups studied at least, bilingualism has no detrimental influence on mental ability. Will this be true always, especially in adulthood? Some people doubt it. Jespersen puts this rhetorical question: 'Has any bilingual child ever developed into a great artist in speech, a poet or orator?' (*Language, Its Nature, Development and Origin*, New York, 1922, p. 148.)

There are a number of people who have expressed themselves in a language not their own and have achieved eminence. As examples may be cited the Renaissance writers who had their vernacular but who wrote in Latin, the German philosopher, Leibnitz, who wrote in French, the Pole, Conrad, who became one of the foremost English writers, Khalil Gibran, and Ernest Dimnet who relinquished his French for English in his literary work. As for bilingual orators, Belgium, Canada, Wales and South Africa would furnish us with the names of many.

in other words, would be among those who would rank in the upper 5 percentile with regard to binguality, because as I pointed out before, I regard proficiency in the second language as the chief determinant of binguality.

STAGE VI. At the top end of this scale of binguality we have, of course, the unapproachable ideal, viz. 100 per cent perfection in both languages. I mention this stage not only for the sake of mere theoretical completeness but also because bilingualism has often been given this meaning by people who, wishing to discountenance any systematic efforts to gain command of both languages, allege the impossibility of becoming 100 per cent proficient in both. Such people are often heard to say: "There is no person who is really bilingual," to which it may be replied that, if 100 percentness is looked for, there are few, if any, completely unilingual people in the world, i.e. people who have reached 100 per cent perfection in one language. Taking English, shall we call the language of Shakespeare, or Milton, or Shelley, or Tennyson, or Coleridge 100 per cent perfect, or not? If not, how shall we grade them? If there is any one of them 100 per cent, how many other such people are there?

It seems to us, therefore, to be either unmitigated nonsense or mere laziness of mind to consider all attempts at becoming bilingual futile merely because there exists in the imagination of some people an unapproachable ideal of perfectibility in both, i.e. an equilingualism of 100 per cent in each.

BILINGUALISM NOT EQUILINGUALISM

From the above it will be clear that bilingualism does not necessarily mean equilingualism. For example, let us look at the following diagram which measures language ability on a scale from 0 to 100. Person A reaches a level of 80 in his mother tongue and 10 in his other tongue. Person B reaches only 10 in each. Which one is the bilingual person? Shall we call B the bilingual person merely because he is *equi*lingual? And A the unilingual person because he is not equilingual? The chances are that neither is bilingual. B is definitely not bilingual merely because he is equally poor in both languages. He is not even lingual by normal adult standards. Of course, he might be a mentally defective adult who just happens to have grown up in a bilingual environment, but we are not now considering exceptional cases. Though equilingual, this person B may not qualify for even the lowest stage of bilingualism outlined above. Take person A. He, at least, is lingual. But whether we call him bilingual or not will depend on how far that 10 per cent ability in his second language takes him towards being a useful citizen of South African society. Actually, it will not take him very far— probably not even far enough to reach Stage I.

Obviously an 80/10 score betokens a much abler person than a 10/10.

Also I would prefer to employ an 80/60 man rather than a 60/60 man. But if I am asked to say whether an 80/40 man is better than a 60/60 man I would say that it entirely depended on the job the man has to perform.

I prefer to look upon language ability as a continuum which varies all the way from a possible zero ability in that function (or functions) to the ideal 100 per cent. It is all a question of degree. The question ought not to be: "Is a man bilingual or not bilingual?" but "How

GRAPH I

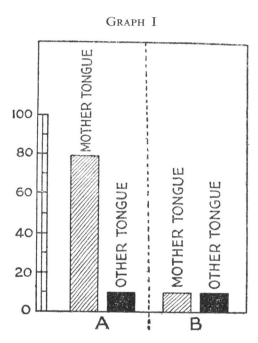

Who is the more bilingual, A or B?

much, or to what extent, is he bilingual?" And this "howmuchness" can be graded like steps on a ladder, depending, as I pointed out before, largely on the purpose for which such bilingualism is required. Failure to distinguish these grades or degrees of bilingualism leads now, as in the past, to confusion in thought and injustice in administration. The Government declared, for example, that after 1928 no civil servant would be appointed who was not fully bilingual. What does "fully bilingual" mean? Is it Stage I or Stage VI? One man who has barely reached Stage I claims that he is fully bilingual and demands appointment, while another, thinking of "fully bilingual" in terms of Stage VI, complains bitterly against authority for demanding the impossible.

C

It is time for us to clarify our concepts on this point, because it is plain to every thinking person that a bilinguality which is adequate for the ordinary purposes of citizenship or for the requirements of a train-conductor may be wholly inadequate for the work of the bilingual teacher, who has not only to inspire young children by talking to them in their mother tongue, but also to serve as a linguistic model for them during the years of immaturity and growth.

COMPLICATING FACTORS

There are a number of complicating factors which cannot be gone into in this limited discussion, as where a knowledge of a special set of technical terms is required for a particular job. Thus, though the general ability to use a language may be identical in the case of two clerks, the one may work in a legal department requiring a knowledge of legal terms and the other may deal with rolling stock on the railways where a totally different set of terms is required. These are to be looked upon as specializations, and can as a rule be mastered without much difficulty because of their relatively circumscribed nature, once the man has a good general knowledge of the language.

For purposes of simplicity, we have confined ourselves in these gradations to a person's general ability in language—the big, common denominator that is used in the communication between all the departments of life. To acquire this takes time. The ability is wide and does not come as the result of merely swotting up a few technical terms or a few grammatical rules. It requires years of actual usage and experience. This must be supplemented and accelerated by the school where facilities for the use of the second language and experience in it must be provided, and where the necessary discipline must also be given in an accurate and happy use of words to express thoughts and feelings.

In conclusion we must stress again the fact that these stages do not represent mere points on the scale with wide gulfs between them. No, they themselves have width and merge into one another like the colour bands on the spectrum. It is all a question of degree. One man may be just over the border of a lower stage, while another may just be verging on the border of the stage above, and yet both will be placed in the same stage. As our knowledge of the subject grows we may be able to subdivide these stages according to the more specific requirements of particular situations. This will become possible when we have devised more accurate yardsticks for measuring language ability than those consisting in the opinions of people, even though they be examiners in school examinations in their existing form. These we know are often notoriously variable in standard from year to year, and the standard is hardly ever the same for the two languages.

The use of standardized tests similar to those which we used in the

Bilingualism Survey (to be described later) has great possibilities, not only in determining a man's fitness for qualifying for a certain stage of bilingualism, but also in assisting in determining accurately what the child's home language is so that he may be taught in his home medium —which is essential in the initial stages of his school career.

CHAPTER II

SCHOOL ORGANIZATION IN RELATION TO LANGUAGE

THE Act of Union in 1910 laid down the principle of equality in language: "Both the English and Dutch (now Afrikaans) languages shall be official languages of the Union, and shall be treated on a footing of equality and enjoy equal freedom, rights and privileges." Almost immediately after the various provinces gave effect to this principle in their school legislation, each in its own way. In what follows we shall describe the position as it is to-day. In doing so, careful distinction must be drawn between (a) the teaching of these languages *as subjects*, and (b) the use of these languages as *media* of instruction in other subjects. Failure to make this simple distinction has been the cause of a good deal of confusion of thought on this subject, not only in South Africa but also in other bilingual countries.[1] This confusion has unfortunately been exploited with a view to misleading the uninitiated. For example, whenever the introduction of the partial use of the second language as a *medium* was mooted, that section of the Press which opposed such a step did everything in its power to make people believe that it meant doing away with the *mother tongue as a subject*. Nothing could be more untrue and misleading. Therefore, at the risk of labouring the obvious, I shall endeavour to explain the status of language (a) as *a subject* and (b) as *a medium* in South Africa.

(a) LANGUAGE AS A SUBJECT. Both languages are taught as subjects in all Government (or public) schools. These are attended by over 95 per cent of South African children. In most private schools, attended by the other 5 per cent, the second language is also taught, though somewhat indifferently as a rule. In the Cape, Orange Free State and Transvaal the second language is taught as a subject to all children, unless the parent objects. Such objections however hardly ever occur. In Natal the 1942 Education Ordinance stipulates that both languages shall be taught as subjects to every pupil from Standard I.

Though the regulations differ somewhat in the four provinces, it can be assumed that all children in South African schools are taught both official languages *as subjects*. This is the general position in a nutshell as far as the legislative requirements are concerned.

Obviously the child begins to learn his first language as a subject right from the start. But when and how a beginning should be made with the study of the second language as a subject becomes a question of educational method.

According to the best educational theory in South Africa to-day

---

[1] Cf. Michael West: *Bingualism*, p. 70.

both official languages should be taught to all pupils as subjects right from the beginning, with the following important provisos: (i) The child must hear the second language first, then learn to speak it, then to read and write it; (ii) the young child must under no circumstances learn to read or write the second language until it can do so in the first language; (iii) it does not matter much how early in school life the child starts with the second language provided that the way of learning it follows the mode of acquisition of the first language. This is best achieved in free association with other children who speak the second language. Failing the presence of such children, the second language should be introduced conversationally through games and other interesting experiences of intrinsically educational value to the child, e.g. simple stories from the field of history, geography, nature study, etc.

Used in this way, the language lesson (whether in the first or the second language) becomes ancillary to the other subjects, instead of being something sterile by itself. Too often, however, these language lessons which occur once a day on the time-table are occupied with absolute drivel as far as the content of the language exercises is concerned. Conversely every lesson, no matter whether it is in arithmetic, history or health, should also be a language lesson in the sense that the teacher should insist on every child's using good clear forms of expression when it speaks about that subject. For slovenliness in language leads to slovenliness in thought—no matter what the subject. There are many experienced teachers who realize this and carry this principle into effect in both official languages, because they find that the time allotted to any one of the two languages as a subject is really too little for them to ensure proficiency in the use of the language, particularly in its spoken form. This brings us to the next point, the use of language as a medium of instruction.

Before we pass on to that, however, it must be noted that there is still a considerable field of experimentation open to determine the optimum stage at which the second language should be started in a formal way; that is, when we should start with reading and spelling in the second language so as to cause as little confusion as possible in the study of the first language. A very comprehensive experiment was planned in collaboration with the Transvaal Education Department by Drs. M. L. Fick and P. A. W. Cook of the National Bureau of Educational and Social Research to investigate this problem over a period of years; but owing to the war it had to be postponed.

(*b*) LANGUAGE AS A MEDIUM. There is no bilingual country in the world where the principle of *home language* medium has been more strongly entrenched in the law of the land in respect of both languages than in South Africa. In general there are four different principles according to which the media of instruction are determined in bilingual (or trilingual) countries.

(*a*) The language of the *home*, or the *family* (*cuius stirps eius lingua*). This we may designate the South African principle, as its consistent application is confined to South Africa.

(*b*) The medium is determined by the *religious allegiance* of the community (*cuius religio eius lingua*), e.g. as in Canada (Quebec), where Roman Catholic children, even from English-speaking homes, as a rule receive their instruction through the French medium.

(*c*) *The Swiss system*, where the child is taught through the language of the *place* (municipality) where he lives, whatever the language of the home of an individual child may be. The school authority in Switzerland is the municipality (not the Federal Government, which is trilingual, nor the government of the Canton, which may also be bilingual or even trilingual). Except in the cities of Fribourg and of Bienne, the Swiss municipalities are not bilingual; they have one language which has remained the same for centuries. Even in a bilingual city like Berne, where about one-third of the inhabitants speak French in their homes, nobody asks for a French medium public school and there are scarcely any private schools to which French-speaking parents might turn if they wished to enjoy the South African principle. In fact, as Prof. Pierre Bovet of Geneva points out, the Swiss principle has become so part and parcel of the local tradition, that an application of the home language medium principle would mean such a revolution that nobody would be found to advocate it.

Belgium presents a combination of the Swiss and the South African principles. The kingdom has been divided into three linguistic areas: (*a*) Wallonie—the French-speaking part; (*b*) the Flemish country where Flemish is spoken; and (*c*) the remainder of the country including Brussels, which is considered a bilingual region. In the last area the South African principle is applied; in the other two the Swiss principle.

(*d*) *The language of the State* (*cuius regio eius lingua*) determines the medium irrespective of the language spoken in individual homes or localities. This is the principle applied consistently in the United States of America. English is the medium of instruction in the public schools throughout, even in Italian, Polish, Swedish and German communities within the U.S.A. The home language of these immigrants is not much bothered about. The language of the State is insisted upon as a medium; for it is regarded as the chief instrument for their Americanization. The argument is that only by having a common means of intercourse can a common spiritual heritage be built up for the American nation, which is still young and fully occupied with the assimilation of a large number of immigrants into her body politic. Applying this same principle to South Africa one should use a bilingual programme of education involving the use of both the State languages as media as an instrument for South Africanization and for laying the basis for building up a common heritage which is truly South African and at the same time unique.

The regulations concerning language as a medium in South Africa are briefly as follows. The child must be taught through the medium of his home language in the primary classes. The parent has no choice in the matter. In the Cape and Orange Free State provinces this compulsion is enforced up to and including Standard VI and in the Transvaal up to and including Standard IV, beyond which the parent has the right to claim that the second language shall be gradually introduced as an additional medium in certain subjects. But this prerogative is seldom exercised in practice. At any rate, the medium of instruction is seldom changed during the child's school course. This is probably due to the recent development of separate, single-medium schools instead of dual-medium schools. In the latter a change-over would be easy. In the former it would mean a change of schools which has an uprooting effect on the child and is not so easily effected.

The Natal regulations are an exception to the compulsory home language medium principle. There the parent may choose the medium right from the beginning (i.e. whether his child is to be instructed through English or Afrikaans as a medium). In 1942, however, a new regulation was passed, which laid down that every pupil above Standard I shall be taught some portion of the curriculum (for not less than one half-hour or more than one hour per day) through the medium of the language which has not been selected by the parents as the medium of instruction.

The practical outcome of these regulations has been that in the three provinces where home language medium is compulsory, nearly 90 per cent of the Afrikaans pupils in the primary classes receive their instruction through their home language as medium. In Natal the proportion is only about 60 per cent, but it is rapidly rising. In each province, however, nearly 100 per cent of the pupils with English as their home language receive their instruction through English. This is just the general picture. Actually the situation is more complex, because, as will be shown in Chapters IV and V below, the home language of South African children is becoming less purely unilingual. A considerable group is growing up where the child's home environment consists of both languages in varying proportions. Consequently the medium may be either language or both.

At any rate in the above figures is to be found the reason why it was the Afrikaans leaders more than the English who were the protagonists of the principle of making the home language medium compulsory. The English section simply took it as axiomatic that their children should be taught through their home language, English. They therefore never felt the need for making it compulsory. That is why in Natal, the most English of the four provinces, the choice is still left to the parents.

Partly as a result of compulsion and the increased status of Afrikaans, the idea of the mother tongue as the medium of instruction has gained so much ground among the Afrikaans-speaking section that it is doubtful whether a change in the law from making it compulsory to leaving it to parental choice will make much difference in actual practice in South Africa in the future—at any rate, not as regards the medium chosen for the child's elementary education. Thus "The law has been our schoolmaster," as St. Paul puts it.[1]

The South African community—particularly the Afrikaans-speaking section—has learnt its lesson. And once a lesson has been ingrained in the mind of a people, the law is no longer essential and we can rely on enlightenment rather than on compulsion.

Having mastered their first lesson and realized the importance of the home language medium principle in the early stages, South Africans now seem ready for their second lesson, to learn the importance of *the bilingual medium principle* in the later stages of the child's school career. And it is a question which might very well be considered whether the time is not ripe for this bilingual medium principle to be enforced by law until such time as it is fully entrenched in practice, when it will be accepted as quite the natural thing in the education of a bilingual citizen in this bilingual country. Whereas in the case of the home language medium principle it was the Afrikaans section chiefly who had to be educated up to it, it will now be chiefly the English section who will have to be educated up to the bilingual medium principle. For it is chiefly in the English schools that there has been a reluctance to introduce Afrikaans as an additional medium in the post-primary classes. Such bilingual medium schools as have been established in the past have grown up chiefly in predominantly Afrikaans communities. It will therefore be a test of the bona fides of the English communities whether they will adopt the bilingual medium principle in their schools.

TYPES OF SCHOOL ORGANIZATION

To meet the demands of these regulations, two main types of school organization have been evolved in the South African educational system: (a) Unilingual medium Schools and (b) Bilingual medium Schools.

Where in the subsequent tables and graphs these two types of schools are contrasted under the abbreviated names of *Unilingual* and *Bilingual*

[1] Galatians iii. 24. In Greek the law is called "paidagogos," i.e., literally, the slave guardian who conducted the young child to school.

schools respectively, these designations must be taken to include all the sub-types outlined here, unless there is a note to the contrary.

(*a*) UNILINGUAL MEDIUM SCHOOLS. Under this arrangement Afrikaans-speaking and English-speaking children go to entirely separate schools where each group receives instruction exclusively through Afrikaans and English respectively. This type of separation is found in the large towns and cities where sufficiency of numbers has warranted the establishment of separate institutions. The second language of course is still learnt *as a subject* and is generally taught by the direct method. These schools are sometimes also called *single medium* or *separate medium schools*. There are primary and secondary as well as high schools of this kind.

(*b*) BILINGUAL MEDIUM SCHOOLS. The bilingual medium school teaches both Afrikaans and English-speaking pupils under the same roof. The law requires that provision be made for the home language by means of parallel classes for any group of not less than 15 pupils in the lower standards; failing this, bilingual teachers must be provided to teach the class through both media. In order to give effect to the regulations which require instruction through the medium of the mother tongue, various types of bilingual medium organization have been devised in accordance with the relative proportions of the two language groups in the school and the level of their scholastic attainment. The following are the chief:

(1) *The Parallel Class System.* Under this system the Afrikaans and English-speaking pupils are taught in separate classes, each receiving instruction through the medium of his home language. If the numbers in the one group are so small that one teacher per class is not warranted, two or more classes are sometimes combined under one teacher. This system is in operation more frequently at the primary level than at the secondary level. It implements, in the primary stage at least, the mother-tongue medium regulation as consistently as the unilingual school, in so far as the formal instruction of individual pupils is concerned.

(2) *The Dual Medium System.* This term has been somewhat indiscriminately applied to describe the following different types of educational practice:

(i) The first is the case in which the teacher uses English and Afrikaans as media alternatively in instructing one class in subjects like history or geography. The English-speaking pupils take notes in English and the Afrikaans-speaking pupils in Afrikaans. Terminology in both languages is thus absorbed. Alternate instruction within the same class takes place when the class contains a minority so small that it is impracticable to constitute a separate class for that minority. The teacher in consequence repeats his English instruction in Afrikaans or vice versa. Though this sometimes occurs in primary classes where instruction is individualized, it is found more frequently in the higher standards. At the time when this investigation took place this system operated at the Cradock Boys' School, and the results achieved were remarkably good. The institutions where this repetition method is used most commonly, however, are the agricultural colleges (especially at Onderstepoort where veterinary officers are trained) and the South African Military College. Its purpose is to be found in the desire to ensure the efficient functioning of the trainees as bilingual Government officials in the bilingual environments to which their duties will inevitably lead them.

(ii) The term "dual medium" is also applied to the practice of teaching certain subjects through the English medium and others through the Afrikaans medium—found particularly at post-primary level.[1] Such practice is considered acceptable where pupils have reached a sufficiently high level of attainment in the second language to make it effective as an additional medium of instruction. This naturally is in addition to instruction in the second language as a subject, almost always taught by the direct method.

(iii) The third type combines the parallel-class and dual-medium systems. A great variety of combinations is possible depending largely on local circumstances, such as the proportion of English and Afrikaans pupils, the qualifications of the teachers and the grade of school. Thus it is quite possible that a school which has parallel classes in the lower standards may develop the dual-medium pattern in the higher standards by increasing progressively the number of subjects taught through the other medium. This seems to be the general pattern to be aimed at where a bilingual community is to be served. In a large school, however, where the proportion of pupils in the two language groups is such that there are fairly large numbers of each kind, the parallel-class system seems to be the only feasible organization *in the early standards*, particularly because of the

---

[1] Compare in this connection the provisions of the so-called *Hertzog Act*, which General Hertzog as Minister of Education introduced in the Orange Free State in 1908. It laid down that up to Standard IV instruction was to be given through the medium of the mother tongue. In classes where there were both English and Afrikaans pupils, both media were to be used and the teacher should be able to pass freely from one medium to the other. The language which was not the medium of instruction was to be introduced gradually into the school course. Above Standard III every child was required to learn both English and Afrikaans as languages, unless special exemption was granted. Above Standard IV at least three principal subjects were to be taught through the medium of English and three through the medium of Dutch.

difficulties of early language instruction, quite apart from other considerations.

As we pointed out above, in the initial stages the first language and the second language have to be studied in different ways. The reading and spelling of the two languages should not be commenced at the same time. Now if the children with different first languages are mixed in fairly large proportions in the same class under one teacher, it will make the rudimentary teaching of the two languages impossible, for the one section of the class must learn the one language formally as its first language, while the other must learn it only conversationally as its second language, and vice versa. While this may be manageable for a teacher where there are only a few in the minority group, it is obviously impracticable where there are fair numbers of each section in a large class under one teacher. Therefore only after a beginning has been made with the formal teaching of both languages does it seem feasible to mix the two sections into one class and use the dual-medium method in one or other of its forms.

THE MAIN ISSUE

The question as to whether the bilingual school should adopt the "parallel class" system or use the "dual medium" method, or should use both systems at different stages within the same school, is really a matter of school method and organization depending, as we pointed out above, on local circumstances, and it is subsidiary to the main issue with which the country is now faced. The main issue is the choice between the *bilingual school* on the one hand and the *unilingual school* on the other as the regular type best fitted to meet the South African situation as a whole.

The bilingual school can be defined as the school (i) where English and Afrikaans-speaking children associate freely together so that they learn to know each other as well as each other's languages; (ii) where the method of instruction is such that every child, no matter what the language of his home or of his schoolmates, is guaranteed to become an educated, bilingual South African citizen.

Though the bilingual school (whichever of the above forms it may take) is considered to present more difficulties of organization and time-table and accommodation, its advocates claim for it several social and educational advantages over the unilingual or separate school. These advantages are held to arise from the fact that the school's environment is enriched by the cultural contributions of both sections. By working and playing together from their early youth, Afrikaans and English-speaking children learn to work together as they will have to do as adults. By hearing the other language spoken at any rate and by having certain common school exercises in the assembly hall (prayers, announcements, etc.) in English and Afrikaans alternately each week, they have greater opportunities for becoming bilingual and for the appreciation of each other's personalities and cultural and social outlook than have children in unilingual schools.

The advocates of the unilingual medium school, on the other hand, state categorically that the social advantages of the bilingual school are questionable and that in the unilingual school children gain a much better understanding of their own history and language and cultivate greater respect for the other section's cultural heritage. Precipitation into one school would not give these advantages as the minority group invariably suffers in the combined school. They claim with equal assertiveness that the unilingual school is sounder pedagogically. While the child may become *au fait* with the second language in the bilingual school (though some of the extreme advocates do not concede even this), their mother tongue suffers. They condemn unequivocally the use of the second language as a medium at any stage. In short, the unilingual medium school is claimed to be more desirable socially and more efficient educationally than the bilingual school.

Unfortunately, most of these claims are made on *a priori* grounds and are not backed by objective data or scientific proof so far as the South African situation is concerned. In fact the vehemence with which they are propounded is generally in inverse proportion to the amount of scientifically reliable data which can be adduced in support of these views. Assertion alone does not necessarily verify a statement. Such little South African evidence as we have for or against these claims usually depends on the rather limited and unsystematic experience of individuals; it will hardly survive the test of scientific analysis.

It must therefore be admitted that, much as we would like certain pet theories to be true, we have argued pretty much in the dark owing to the paucity of facts on these issues as far as South Africa is concerned. For such facts as have been adduced from pedagogical experience in other countries are often not applicable to education in South Africa because of the dissimilarity of conditions. As the result, however, of a Survey on Bilingualism which will be described in the next chapter, we have now been placed in possession of a set of data which, though not by any means complete, will enable us to draw conclusions with a degree of reliability not hitherto possible. To what extent some of the above-mentioned claims are justified or not—in the South African context—will be considered in the light of data which will be presented in subsequent chapters.

CHAPTER III

THE MEASUREMENT OF BILINGUALISM
(THE 1938 SURVEY)

IN 1938, while still Director of the National Bureau for Educational and Social Research, I undertook an extensive survey of bilingualism in the schools of South Africa. Before doing so a study was made of research work conducted in all the countries in the world where any scientific investigations had been made on bilingualism.

PURPOSE OF SURVEY

The purpose of this survey was four-fold, to study:

(1) The *degree of bilingualism* attained by children from the primary school to the completion of the secondary school and the relative rates of development in the mother tongue and the other tongue under different environmental and school conditions. This was done by an elaborate series of language tests in English and Afrikaans.

(2) The *factors* which determine linguistic growth in the child throughout his school career, e.g.:

(*a*) Individual or personal, such as the child's native *intelligence*. This was done by means of intelligence tests. Some of these tests were of a non-linguistic nature.

(*b*) Factors connected with the child's *home environment*, e.g.:
  (i) The language used by father, mother, brothers, sisters, etc.
  (ii) The cultural influences of the home, such as the books available, radio, etc.
  (iii) The economic status of the home.
  (iv) The attitude of the home towards the other language group and its culture and institutions.

(*c*) *Extra-home influences*, such as the church, cinema, sports, the child's friends, and organizations like the Boy Scouts, Voortrekkers, etc.

(*d*) *School influences*.
  (i) The efficacy of the language instruction, e.g. the qualifications of the teachers and the methods used.
  (ii) The attitude of the staff and chiefly of the principal towards the second language and the language groups in the school.
  (iii) The use of adjuvants, such as the school library, assembly exercises, and debating societies.

    (iv) The type of school organization; viz. whether unilingual medium or bilingual (i.e. parallel or dual) medium.

(3) The *influence of the medium* on:

    (*a*) The pupil's attainment in Afrikaans and English.

    (*b*) The pupil's progress in the other school subjects.

    (*c*) The pupil's general mental development, as reflected by intelligence tests.

(4) The degree to which lack of knowledge in one or both official languages affected the chances of employment and *vocational advancement* of young people after leaving school. This was, *inter alia*, done by a study of the records kept by Juvenile Affairs' Boards and by correspondence with large employers of juvenile labour.

SCOPE OF SURVEY

This survey covered 18,773 pupils in primary and high schools of the Transvaal (12,634), the Cape (3,933) and Natal (2,206). The standards actually tested were IV to X inclusive. Twelve standardized tests suitable for that range of pupil were used in all. These tests were given in schools selected in consultation with the respective Education Departments, in such a way as to be more or less representative of the chief types to be found in the three provinces. Owing to the advent of the war the investigation could not be extended to the Orange Free State as well and the tabulation of the results had to be stopped.

Nevertheless this investigation was acclaimed by all the leading authorities on bilingualism with whom we had been in contact, either personally or through correspondence in various parts of the world, as by far the most comprehensive and thoroughgoing investigation on bilingualism hitherto conducted. This was made possible by generous grants received from Carnegie funds administered by the South African Council for Educational and Social Research. Throughout this investigation I enjoyed the able assistance of my colleagues in the National Bureau for Educational and Social Research, especially of the following: Dr. M. L. Fick, Dr. P. A. W. Cook, Dr. Felix Brummer, Miss K. Henshall and Miss B. J. Versfeld. In the field I was assisted by inspectors of schools. Among them I must specially mention the names of Inspector C. M. Booysen (now Secretary) of the Natal Education Department and Inspector S. Hobson of the Cape Education Department.

In addition to giving the standardized scholastic and intelligence tests mentioned above (which involved at least two days for a single group), we obtained for each child a complete case history reflecting the child's socio-economic and cultural background. The teachers filled in long questionnaires regarding the facilities provided by the school, such as extra reading matter, debating societies, etc. The results of the tests were analysed statistically according to age, standard, intelligence quotient, economic environment, type of school organization, etc. in order to make sure, before coming to any conclusion regarding any particular point, that the other things were equal. For example, most unilingual Afrikaans-speaking children grow up in the remote rural areas where they are subject not only to cultural isolation but also to low economic standards. The unilingual English-speaking pupils on the other hand are found in large urban areas where, while they may not all be economically well off, they are exposed to a much wider variety of experiences and opportunities for linguistic and mental development. The achievements of these two groups would obviously not be comparable. In order, therefore, to find comparable groups we had to go to areas such as Bathurst (Albany) district to find unilingual English-speaking children who lived in a rural and more or less equally isolated and economically backward environment with whom to compare the unilingual Afrikaans-speaking children from isolated and poor rural areas.

There has been found to be in South Africa a very close correlation between economic status and the average intelligence of a community. So before comparing different types of schools, e.g. English or Afrikaans, unilingual or bilingual schools respectively, one had to make sure that the other important factors (e.g. intelligence level and economic environment) were also comparable. The investigation was therefore an extremely complex one. It was only by dealing with large numbers, such as were covered in this survey, that anything like the semblance of a scientific basis for our conclusions could be arrived at. Though thousands of tables and graphs have already been worked out, this investigation has not yet been completed owing to interruption by the war. It is hoped, however, to complete it when the war is over and publish a full report.

TWO PARTICULAR ASPECTS

During the last few years, however, two aspects of the problem as outlined above have roused a good deal of attention in the press and in the minds of parents who wish to do the right thing by their children's education. Moreover, in the absence of objective data, a good deal of confusion of thought seems to be evident in these matters. More heat than light has been generated in consequence. I have, therefore, decided to present a few of the preliminary conclusions arrived at at this stage of the investigation with a view to throwing some light on these problems. I refer, in the first place, to point (2) (*d*) under *School Influences*: viz. a comparison between the relative achievements of pupils in unilingual and in bilingual schools respectively. The second point is No. (3) above, viz. the influence of the medium on the child's progress in school and on his general mental development; that is, what happens when a child receives part or whole of his instruction through the medium of his second language. These two points are obviously related.

In this very limited preliminary report it is obviously not possible to submit all the masses of figures and graphs on which our main findings are based. Also, we shall have to confine ourselves to giving only the chief figures and general conclusions in so far as they are relevant to the two problems as stated above. Minor points, however interesting they may be, have of necessity to be omitted.

TESTS OF LANGUAGE ABILITY

It was essential in this survey to have an objective measure of language ability, i.e. one that does not vary with the person measuring. Moreover the measures must be comparable between the two languages. For example, a score of x points in Afrikaans and of x points in English must denote an equal proficiency in each. Language ability is, however, so wide and involves so many factors that at the present stage of scientific measurement we have not yet reached objective measures for all these factors. For example, as regards correctness of speech and accent we shall probably for some time still have to rely on the judgment of individuals. The more experienced they are in applying oral tests and the better their judgment, the more reliable such measures will be.

There are, however, aspects which lend themselves more readily to objective measurement, and in most of these standardized tests and scales already exist in English and in Afrikaans. I mention a few:

(a) *Range of vocabulary.* This is of primary importance as an indication of language proficiency, especially at the lower stages demanded for a second language. This is something which grows only with experience in the language and with its active use in reading, writing and speaking. It cannot be swotted up like rules from a grammar book. Nor is it dependent upon the knowledge of a particular prescribed book. It is fundamental, and from our use of vocabulary tests of thousands of South African children we have found it the best single indication of their proficiency in English and Afrikaans respectively, even in the spoken form. The average adult has about 11,000 words in his mother tongue. These are the words he understands. In speaking he uses less, and in writing still less, of course. My own estimate is that a person with vocabulary range of at least 3,000–4,000 words which he understands in the second language, ought to qualify for Stage I mentioned in Chapter I. There are already a variety of such tests in English and Afrikaans and we have used them extensively in measuring the vocabulary range of school pupils and university students as well as the general cultural level of whole communities.

(b) *Ability to understand what is read.* There exists a variety of tests which measure both speed of reading and comprehension in English and Afrikaans.

(c) *Composition and power of expression.* Scales exist in English by use of which a subjective matter like composition, style, etc. can be objectively measured, that is by which independent judges rarely vary in their scores of individual essays. Afrikaans scales are not fully standardized as yet.

(d) There are *spelling* tests in English and Afrikaans, but this factor is of far less importance than the other three. The advantages of these tests over the ordinary school examinations can be summed up as follows: (1) They are objective. (2) They are accurate and reliable. (3) They are quick and easy to apply. (4) They have a wide range, since the same test can be used to test pupils in the lower standards of the primary school as well as students in the university. We have norms for each standard. (5) They test the fundamentals of language, i.e. the cumulative results of the actual use of the language. One cannot "swot up" for them overnight.

By combining the results of a number of these different types of test and giving each its appropriate weight in the total, we were able to evolve a fairly reliable index of language ability in each of the two official languages. But before dealing with these results we shall first explain how we arrived at an objective measure of the child's home background as regards language. This will be done in the next chapter.

D

CHAPTER IV

THE MEANING OF "HOME LANGUAGE"

THE most important part of the chid's linguistic experience outside the school is gained in the home. In order to gauge this more accurately than is often done by merely asking the child what his home language is, the following questions were put to each child tested and their completion was supervised item by item. These questions constitute part of a long list comprising an *Information Test*. (The questions are given the numbers they had in this test.) Other questions elicited the names of books, magazines and newspapers which were read in the child's home; the frequency with which he went to the talkies; the names of the principal towns he had visited as well as lived in for more than a year at a time, etc. These questions were designed to give as complete a picture as possible of the child's linguistic environment.

21. Which language do you hear most at home? ....

22. (*a*) Does your *father* speak to you in AFRIKAANS?
Underline: (1) Always. (2) Often. (3) Sometimes. (4) Never.

(*b*) Does your *mother* speak to you in AFRIKAANS?
Underline: (1) Always. (2) Often. (3) Sometimes. (4) Never.

(*c*) Do your *brothers and sisters* (if any) speak to you in AFRIKAANS?
Underline: (1) Always. (2) Often. (3) Sometimes. (4) Never.

(*d*) Do you hear AFRIKAANS on the school playground?
Underline: (1) Always. (2) Often. (3) Sometimes. (4) Never.

(*e*) Do you speak AFRIKAANS on the school playground?
Underline: (1) Always. (2) Often. (3) Sometimes. (4) Never.

23. (*a*) Does your *father* speak to you in ENGLISH?
Underline: (1) Always. (2) Often. (3) Sometimes. (4) Never.

(*b*) Does your *mother* speak to you in ENGLISH?
Underline: (1) Always. (2) Often. (3) Sometimes. (4) Never.

(*c*) Do your *brothers and sisters* (if any) speak to you in ENGLISH?
Underline: (1) Always. (2) Often. (3) Sometimes. (4) Never.

24. Which language do your parents consider the more important for you to know, English or Afrikaans? ....

25. Which language do your three best friends speak to you?

(*a*) ....

(*b*) ....

(*c*) ....

26. What other languages do you speak besides English and Afrikaans?

....

27. Have you a wireless set in your home? ....
    Which language do your parents prefer to hear on the wireless?

    ....

    You? ....

28. To which church do your parents belong: an English or a Dutch church...

29. Do you go to Sunday School? .... If so, do they speak English or Afrikaans to you there? ....

It was stressed that if "always" was underlined for English "never" had to be underlined for Afrikaans, and so on, otherwise the evidence would be self-contradictory.

Certain parents, however, desirous of keeping their child in a particular school, have been known to declare their home language to be different from what it really is. In spite of this, there is every reason to believe that the information gained by these questions reflects the actual situation fairly accurately. It would be a rare thing for a child to falsify all the replies systematically in order to hide the fact that he was in the wrong medium.

The following "weights" were given to the various items underlined in order to determine more specifically the child's *home* language:

	Always	Often	Sometimes	Never
(a) Father ..	3	2	1	0
(b) Mother ..	6	4	2	0
(c) Brothers and Sisters ..	3	2	1	0

To a certain extent these weightings are arbitrary. They were, however, arrived at after some experimentation with various values. The mother was given twice the weighting of the father because it was felt that in most cases the language of the mother is the strongest factor in the home determining the language of the children. After all we speak of our *mother* tongue. The total weight, showing the language heard at home, whether English or Afrikaans, would in each case amount to 12 points. For example, a child who never hears Afrikaans at home would receive a total of $3 + 6 + 3 = 12$ for English. If his father were to speak Afrikaans to him "sometimes" his score would be 11 English 1 Afrikaans. If his brothers and sisters also speak Afrikaans to him sometimes his score would be 10 English and 2 Afrikaans. The two scores will always be complementary, 6 and 6 indicating a complete balance between the two languages heard at home. In cases where the child's father or mother had died too early for the child to be influenced markedly by his or her home language, or if the child had no "brothers and sisters," the amounts of both languages heard in the home were reduced by mathematical proportion so that the total again was 12.

Where the children underlined words (as they sometimes but very rarely did), the values of which were *not* complementary, the replies obtained from the other questions dealing with the child's home environment, church affiliation, etc. were taken into account in adjusting the figures so that the child would be as nearly as possible in his correct language group. These categories in any case show a high correlation with the results of the standardized tests of the child's actual proficiency in English and Afrikaans respectively.

In this way the linguistic structure of the child's home environment was measured on a scale of 12 units. As this makes the tabulation too detailed, we have for convenience grouped these units into *seven* categories or groups, (*a*), (*b*), (*c*), etc., as follows, e.g.:

$$(a) = 0 \text{ English, 12 Afrikaans.} \quad (b) = \left\{ \begin{array}{l} 1 \text{ English, 11 Africaans.} \\ 2 \text{ English, 10 Afrikaans.} \end{array} \right.$$

and so on, as shown in the table below, which groups the 18,773 children tested in the Cape, Natal and Transvaal schools according to the linguistic background of their home environment.

LINGUISTIC STRUCTURE OF HOME ENVIRONMENT OF PUPILS TESTED[1]

		No. of Pupils	Percentage	
(*a*) Afrikaans unilingual (0 Eng. 12 Afr)		4,736	25	
(*b*) Afrikaans unilingual with slight English { 1 Eng. 11 Afr. 2 Eng. 10 Afr. }		2,165	12	37
(*c*) Afrikaans bilingual { 3 Eng. 9 Afr. 4 Eng. 8 Afr. }		2,333	12	
(*d*) Bilingual (50–50) { 5 Eng. 7 Afr. 6 Eng. 6 Afr. 7 Eng. 5 Afr. }		828	5	23
(*e*) English bilingual { 8 Eng. 4 Afr. 9 Eng. 3 Afr. }		1,165	6	
(*f*) English unilingual with slight Afrikaans { 10 Eng. 2 Afr. 11 Eng. 1 Afr. }		1,502	8	40
(*g*) English unilingual (12 Eng. 0 Afr.)		6,044	32	
Total No. of Pupils Tested		18,773	100	

[1] The totals in this table should be kept in mind when reading the test results in Chapters V, VI, VII and VIII, as they will not be repeated there owing to lack of space.

The above table is of extreme importance in considering the medium question. It shows very clearly that the home language of South African children is not exclusively English on the one hand, or exclusively Afrikaans on the other hand, as is tacitly assumed by many people who advocate unilingual or single medium schools. The actual facts are that we have between these two extremes—group (a) with 25 per cent exclusively Afrikaans home language and group (g) with 32 per cent exclusively English home language—over 40 per cent of South African children whose home language is both English and Afrikaans in varying degrees and for whom, if the principle of home language medium is logically applied, instruction should really be given through both languages, in varying degrees—in other words, dual-medium instruction—otherwise the so-called sacred principle of home language (or mother tongue) medium would be violated.

The logical application of this principle runs counter to the general application of the system of unilingual or single medium schools in South Africa. For according to this system South African children should go only to one or the other of these two types of single medium schools. The question then arises: What practice should be followed as regards medium for the intermediate zones comprising the children falling in categories (b) to (f) inclusive? It would seem that the dual-medium form of instruction is the only justifiable system for this group, if one starts from the assumption that the principle of home language medium must be applied with absolute consistency throughout the child's school career.

It will be seen, however, from the data which will follow that South African conditions are so complex, and the language background of South African children is so much a matter of degree, that a blind application of an abstract principle based on all-or-none assumptions simply will not work in practice, particularly if the good of the individual child and of the community constitute the main criteria.

The following are a few detailed points of interest in the above table:

(a) There are more unilingual English homes (32 per cent) than unilingual Afrikaans homes (25 per cent). Also, there are relatively twice as many Afrikaans homes in which a little English is heard as English homes in which a little Afrikaans is heard. These data tally with the Census figures.

(b) If one groups together these categories in three main groups, one can say roughly that:

　(i) 37 per cent of the pupils come from more or less *unilingual Afrikaans* homes.

　(ii) 23 per cent of the pupils come from more or less *bilingual* homes.

(iii) 40 per cent of the pupils come from more or less *unilingual English* homes.

These percentages will, of course, vary according to where one draws the lines demarcating the groups.

GRAPH II

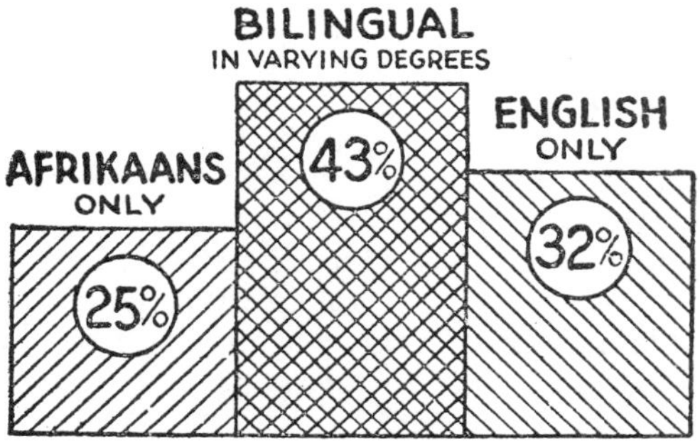

South African pupils divided according to HOME LANGUAGE.
(N.B.—Those with bilingual homes constitute by far the largest group.)

It must be pointed out, however, that the above figures refer to *home* environment only. If one takes into account also the environment outside the home, one finds that there are many children who, while they hear nothing, or relatively little, of the other language spoken by the family members of their home, nevertheless have playmates who speak the other language, or come into contact with the other language (outside the school) in other ways than their homes. Actually, therefore, the proportion of children with a bilingual background (apart from school) is larger than the above figures would indicate. Incidentally, if the Orange Free State had been included in this survey, the proportion of bilingual children shown in the above table would have been bigger. From early years that province has had the reputation for being the most bilingual of the four provinces. In 1908 General Hertzog, who was then Minister of Education for the Orange Free State, introduced the system of dual-medium instruction into the schools.

NOTE ON CENSUS DATA

The following figures are based on the 1936 Union Census in which the number of people (*a*) able to speak both English and Afrikaans, (*b*) English only, (*c*) Afrikaans only, and (*d*) neither, were tabulated.

In the following table, (*d*) was omitted as it was almost negligibly small.

BILINGUALISM AS TO PROVINCES

Percentage of Population Speaking Official Language

	Cape	Natal	Trans-vaal	Orange Free State	Total
(*a*) Both English and Afrikaans ...	66	44	66	69	64
(*b*) English only ...	15	53	18	3	19
(*c*) Afrikaans only ...	18	2	15	28	16

The Orange Free State (69 per cent) is the most bilingual of the four provinces and Natal (44 per cent) the least. While 53 per cent of Natal's people speak only English, 28 per cent of the Orange Free State people speak only Afrikaans. Cape and Transvaal are equally bilingual, 66 per cent speaking both. The most bilingual towns in South Africa are Bloemfontein, 75 per cent, and Pretoria, 73 per cent. The most unilingual towns are Durban, 33 per cent, Pietermaritzburg, 42 per cent, and East London, 51 per cent. All other large towns have 60 per cent and over of their population speaking both official languages. (The whole Witwatersrand area with 60 per cent is counted together as a large urban area. Johannesburg by itself has 57 per cent speaking both languages.)

GRAPH III

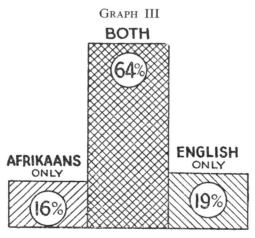

Percentage of Union population able to speak OFFICIAL LANGUAGES (1936 Census). Note the size of the group speaking both official languages. (The percentage speaking neither has been omitted, as it is very small.)

It will be noted that the highest degree of bilingualism is to be found in those provinces and large towns where the majority of the population is Afrikaans-speaking, and the lowest where the majority is English-speaking. The latter group seem to be becoming increasingly aware of their deficiency in this respect and in some quarters they are taking definite steps to improve their bilingualism; thus in Natal the Education Department has recently embarked upon the organization of bilingual schools in order to increase the occasions and opportunities for English-speaking children to come into contact with and actually use Afrikaans.

CHAPTER V

HOME LANGUAGE AS THE MEDIUM OF INSTRUCTION

THE different home language groups shown in the table in the previous chapter were next split up according to the medium through which the children were actually taught in each class or standard at the time the tests were given (irrespective of the medium of the school), in order to ascertain to what extent the principle of home language medium was actually applied in our schools. The results are given below for Standards IV to X combined. The medium categories in the top horizontal line refer to the medium generally used in the standard as a whole:

(a) *Afrikaans* means wholly or predominantly in Afrikaans.
(b) *Both English and Afrikaans* means in more or less equal proportions.
(c) *English* means wholly or predominantly in English.

TABLE SHOWING MEDIUM OF INSTRUCTION IN RELATION TO HOME LANGUAGE[1]

Standards IV–X Combined: 18,773 *Cases*

Home Language	Medium (Percentages)			
	Afrikaans	Both	English	Total
(a) Afrikaans unilingual ...	85·5	9·3	5·2	100·0
(b) Afrikaans unilingual with slight English ...	83·2	7·9	8·9	100·0
(c) Afrikaans bilingual ...	76·0	10·0	14·0	100·0
(d) Bilingual (50/50) ...	44·8	5·4	49·8	100·0
(e) English bilingual ...	8·3	5·2	86·5	100·0
(f) English unilingual with slight Afrikaans ...	2·6	3·6	93·8	100·0
(g) English unilingual ...	0·3	2·1	97·6	100·0
Total ...	43·4	6·0	50·6	100·0

The following are the main points to be noted in the above table:

[1] The percentages in this table, if taken in conjunction with the table on page 46 in the previous chapter, give an indication of the sizes of the groups, the test results of which are given in the subsequent chapters.

(1) Of group (*a*), i.e. those with *completely unilingual Afrikaans environment*, it will be noted that 85·5 per cent received instruction through Afrikaans medium; 9·3 per cent through both, and 5·2 per cent through English medium. This is the one extreme.

(2) At the other extreme we have group (*g*) with *completely unilingual English environment*. Here 97·6 per cent receive their instruction through English medium, 2·1 per cent through both and only 0·3 per cent through Afrikaans.

(3) From these two sets of figures it will be seen that the percentage of Afrikaans unilingual children who receive their instruction through the "wrong" medium, though only 5·2 per cent and much smaller than is generally believed, is seventeen times as great as the percentage of English unilingual children who receive their instruction through the "wrong" medium. The effect of this wrong medium on the educational progress of this group will be shown later.

It should be noted that we are dealing here with the average figures for Standards IV to X combined. If one takes the figures for the *primary* classes only, the percentage of Afrikaans unilingual pupils receiving instruction through their home language is over 90 per cent. In the *high school* standards this percentage drops down into the 80's because here a much higher percentage receive their instruction through both media (e.g.: in the Transvaal high school standards 15 per cent Afrikaans *unilingual* and 6 per cent English *unilingual* pupils receive their instruction through both media more or less equally.) The provinces differ, as will be seen if one compares the Cape and the Transvaal as regards the medium of the two extreme unilingual groups (*a*) and (*g*). While there are relatively less Afrikaans pupils in the Cape primary standards who receive their instruction through the medium of English only than in the Transvaal (Cape, 3 per cent; Transvaal, 7 per cent), the former province uses both media in the primary school much more frequently. Thus while 20 per cent Afrikaans and 4·2 per cent English primary pupils receive instruction through both media in the Cape, practically none in Transvaal primary classes are taught through both media.

Owing to lack of space all the detailed tables cannot be given here.

(4) Having now looked at the two extreme end groups, (*a*) and (*g*), of the above table, let us study the intermediate groups. As one goes down the table from (*a*) to (*g*) and looks at the left-hand column, one notices how the percentage of children receiving Afrikaans medium instruction decreases steadily as they hear less and less Afrikaans and more and more English at home. The opposite is noticed in the right-hand column showing how the percentages of those receiving English medium instruction increase as one goes from group (*a*) to (*g*). On the whole it would be true to say that as far as the unilingual groups are concerned, the principle of home-language medium has been consistently carried into effect in the great majority of cases.

The most interesting point, however, in the above table is the medium used in the case of the middle (bilingual) group (*d*). Here we see that of the children who hear English and Afrikaans almost equally often in their homes, 45 per cent receive their school instruction through Afrikaans medium, 50 per cent through English medium and 5 per cent through both. For the children of this central group it was probably a toss-up as to which of the two media they were put into. It would seem, however, that the bilingual school with dual-medium instruction would, in the case of the bilingual groups (*c*), (*d*) and (*e*), have given expression much more truly to the principle of home language medium than the unilingual class (or school) system into which most of these children had been forced.

(5) The main point that emerges from the above table is that in the case of a very considerable number of school-children in South Africa the home language consists of both English and Afrikaans in varying proportions. The variation of these proportions between home and home, and child and child, is a matter of degree because, as we saw above, linguistic experience is a continuum. To assume, therefore, as has been the tendency amongst certain people of late, that the whole school population is made up only of the two Simon Pure extreme groups, (*a*) and (*g*), with unilingual home environments—when in actual fact the two together comprise only a little more than half of the total, and to advocate on this assumption the building-up of two separate unilingual school systems, is to be guilty of a blindness to what is a very important *fact* in our cultural and social life in South Africa. What is more, these intermediate and central groups, (*b*), (*c*), (*d*), (*e*) and (*f*), are becoming progressively more numerous as bilingualism develops and young people are free to meet each other, to fall in love, and to marry, irrespective of linguistic backgrounds.

One of the main criteria of the adequacy of the school system of a country is the extent to which it reflects the life of the people as a whole. This criterion would be violated if we insisted on unilingual schools being made of universal application in South Africa. There are some, of course, who regard the mixing of the two European sections as an undesirable growth in South African life and have tried, and are still trying, to check it by artificial means. In the past this separatist tendency was strongest amongst the English-speaking section. As figures show, it was the Afrikaans child who frequently attended an English medium school or class, but an English-speaking child rarely attended an Afrikaans medium school. In recent years this separatism has become very marked among the Afrikaans-speaking section. In fact, our figures show that this tendency is stronger among student teachers from the Afrikaans medium normal colleges than among those from the English medium normal college in the Transvaal.[1]

---

[1] See Chapter IX below where this matter is more fully dealt with.

(6) Lastly, it is clear from the above that it is erroneous to imply, as is often done, that when the second language is used as a medium (as it is sometimes used in the post-elementary stage), that the children are being taught through a foreign medium. Afrikaans is not foreign to South African children. Neither is English. And to use either of these languages as a medium of instruction in South African schools is not the same as using French as a medium of instruction in schools in England, simply because it is studied as a subject by English school-children. The situations are by no means parallel.

CHAPTER VI

THE EFFECT OF THE "WRONG" MEDIUM ON EDUCATIONAL PROGRESS

IN order to study the effect of the "wrong" medium on educational progress we first took the extreme case of that small number (5 per cent) of the pupils in group (a)[1] who came from unilingual Afrikaans homes and who received all their schooling exclusively through English, i.e. the "wrong" medium. We then compared their progress with that of the 85·5 per cent of the unilingual Afrikaans home language group who received instruction through their home language. A study of the converse situation, where English pupils from group (g)[1] received their instruction through Afrikaans medium, was not possible, as there were too few such cases to yield statistically significant results. Next we compared the scholastic achievement of these "wrong" medium pupils with that of the subsequent groups, (b), (c), etc. of the table on p. 46 above.

As it is not possible owing to lack of space to give all the results of the numerous tests for all these groups, we give here only the main conclusions regarding the effect of the "wrong" medium on (a) the learning of the two languages as subjects and on (b) their progress in the "content" subjects, e.g. geography and arithmetic.

(a) EFFECT ON ATTAINMENT IN ENGLISH AND AFRIKAANS. If one adds together the scores obtained in English and Afrikaans, the combined score by this "wrong" medium group is appreciably higher than that of Afrikaans unilingual pupils taught exclusively through Afrikaans medium on the one hand and of the English pupils taught exclusively through English medium on the other hand.

EFFECT OF "WRONG" MEDIUM ON SCORES IN ENGLISH AND AFRIKAANS

	Afrikaans Pupils in English Medium	English Pupils in English Medium	Afrikaans Pupils in Afrikaans Medium	English Pupils in Afrikaans Medium (too few to be significant)
Afrikaans Score	468	341	488	(470)
English Score	468	506	352	(430)
Total ...	936	847	840	(900)

[1] See Table on page 46, Chapter IV.

As a concrete illustration we give here the combined "standard" scores obtained in all the Afrikaans and English tests respectively by pupils at the Standard VI stage, where a level of equal proficiency in both languages was reached by the "wrong" medium group. By being taught exclusively through a medium other than their home language (viz. through English) pupils with unilingual Afrikaans home background lose about one-third of a year in Afrikaans. On the other hand, they gain two years in their second language, English.

The relative levels of the two constituent language scores can be visualized in the accompanying graph. The figures given in the last column are not reliable because of the fewness of the cases in that category. The probable errors of the averages are too great to warrant any conclusion. In the other categories the numbers are large and all the differences statistically significant. What is more, the standard scores are comparable from one language to the other. Lack of space precludes a detailed discussion of these results.

GRAPH IV

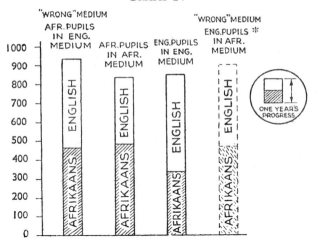

✳ TOO FEW CASES TO BE SIGNIFICANT

Graph showing effect of "wrong" medium on language achievement in English and Afrikaans by Standard VI pupils. By "wrong" medium is meant when pupils from a purely unilingual home environment are taught through medium of the other language. Those taught through the "wrong" medium are in total language achievement nearly one year ahead of those taught through home language medium.

The higher degree of bilingualism reached by the "wrong" medium group is a not unexpected result. It has been borne out by empirical observation of the results of "wrong" medium instruction over many years in our educational history. While this higher degree of bilingualism is not an undesirable result by itself, the question arises: Has this not been attained at the expense of progress in the content subjects?

(*b*) EFFECT ON CONTENT SUBJECTS. A study of the handicap of having to learn content subjects through a medium which is not the home language yields the following general conclusions:

(1) Where the medium is the other language, children with a completely unilingual home background undoubtedly suffer an initial handicap in the learning process with regard to "content" subjects (other than language), e.g. arithmetic, geography, history, etc.

(2) This handicap is more marked at the elementary stage than later.

(3) The handicap is almost precisely in proportion to the relative strangeness of the language used as medium and is practically non-existent where the child's knowledge of the second language approximates to that of his first language—a situation which one finds in groups (*c*), (*d*) and (*e*).

(4) The handicap in a subject like arithmetic, where language plays a relatively small role, is less than in the case of subjects like history and geography, where language plays a bigger role. For example, our tests showed that in the case of arithmetic at the Standard IV stage the children taught through the "wrong" medium are, on an average, about three months behind those taught through the mother-tongue medium, whereas in geography they are nearly $1\frac{1}{2}$ years behind.

(5) The most interesting fact that the tests brought to light was that this handicap is not permanent—even for the extreme (*a*) group. It diminishes as the pupil goes to higher standards. For example, the handicap in arithmetic (i.e. proficiency in mechanical arithmetic and in problem solving) vanishes entirely by the time the pupil gets to Standard VI. That is, by the time they get to the end of the primary school, the children who have had their schooling through the medium of the other tongue do, on an average, just as well as those who had all their schooling up to that stage through their mother tongue.

An even more striking diminution of the initial handicap is observed in the case of geography. By the time the pupil gets to Standard V the handicap has diminished to one year, while in Standard VI it has diminished to four months. By Standard VII it has disappeared completely.

(6) Following this comparison to the higher standards one finds the rather remarkable result that the Afrikaans home language children, who receive their geography instruction through English (i.e. the "wrong") medium, gradually outstrip those who receive their geography instruction through Afrikaans (i.e. the mother-tongue) medium. In Standard VIII the "wrong medium" group are *one* quarter ahead, in Standard IX a little over *two* quarters and by Standard X *four* quarters ahead. It is not easy from the data to hand to account completely for this rather unexpected phenomenon. If the investigation had

originally been planned to cover such a contingency, it might have been possible to give a full explanation. Further studies are needed to follow up this point. The following are suggested as likely factors:

(a) The "wrong" medium group were in the upper standards slightly higher in intelligence (as shown by the intelligence test results) than the "right" medium group. This difference in intelligence is too slight, however, to account for the whole difference in the geography results.

(b) The instruction given to the wrong medium group may have been more efficient. I say "may have been" as the ability of the teachers for these respective groups was not assessed by itself apart from these test results. The chances are, however, strong that for these Afrikaans children who received their schooling through the English medium there was available a much wider variety of reading matter and illustrative material, e.g. maps, travel books, magazines like the *National Geographic*, etc., than for those Afrikaans pupils receiving their instruction exclusively through the Afrikaans medium. Publications of this nature in Afrikaans are very limited in comparison with those available in English, which has behind it the educational and publicity resources of Great Britain, America and the rest of the English-speaking world.

Support for this theory is to be found in the fact that English pupils taught through the medium of English do better as a group in geography than Afrikaans pupils taught through the medium of Afrikaans. Their superiority varies from about one term in the primary standards to three-quarters of a year in the secondary standards. It should be noted that throughout this survey the tests were always given to the pupils in the medium through which they usually received their instruction.

(7) However that may be, the following general conclusion emerges from the facts obtained in this investigation: Taking conditions as they are found in South Africa, where most children have experience with the second language, the school child, if placed in the "wrong" medium suffers an initial but not very serious handicap in his "content" subjects, but as he progresses to higher standards the medium seems to become of decreasing significance and has no observable adverse effect on his learning process. There are exceptions, but this is the total average result.

To go into the probable reasons for this phenomenon might prove a very interesting psychological speculation. It may, for example, be advanced that, once concepts come to have more or less fixed meanings, the labels one gives to them (i.e. the medium) seem to have relatively less significance in the learning process. Whether this theory is true or not cannot be argued here owing to lack of space.

It would have been interesting if an investigation under similarly controlled conditions could have been extended to University levels. This should still be done. But it would seem, to judge from every-day observations of a more or less empirical and casual nature, that a study of University education in this and other countries does not offer evidence of the disastrous effects which higher learning, obtained through a medium other than the student's mother tongue, is alleged to have on the learning process of those who through choice or force of circumstance pursue their University education through that medium. It is probable that there were compensating factors which more than made good any possible loss.

University study has since its earliest beginnings been an international affair, where the medium of instruction was a more or less irrelevant consideration. Latin was in early days the medium of University study, and the foundations of our modern science and arts (including literature) were laid by men who had their University education through the "wrong" medium. Students went where the real masters were and did not bother much about medium. Even in modern times the Universities of Europe have teemed with students from foreign countries. Most of our best professional men—our lawyers, doctors and even our poets and *literati*—have gone for advanced study to countries where the medium was not their own home language. And it would take a bold man to state categorically that because of their having had to study through what was to them a foreign medium (far more foreign than English and Afrikaans are to Afrikaans and English-speaking students respectively in our own country) they are as a group to-day inferior to those professional men who studied exclusively through the medium of their home language.

This is, however, merely an empirical observation for which we are not yet in a position to advance proof of an objective and statistical nature one way or the other. There are besides always factors, such as selection, which affect the situation, and where these are not statistically controlled proof absolute is lacking. We should prefer in this study to confine ourselves to objectively measurable data, such as those collected in the case of these 18,000 pupils in South African schools, drawing our conclusions exclusively from them.

In the next chapter we shall see what happens in cases where children in the bilingual school receive only *part* of their instruction through the medium of their second language.

E

CHAPTER VII

SCHOLASTIC ACHIEVEMENT IN UNILINGUAL AND BILINGUAL SCHOOLS

IN the previous chapter we dealt with the rather extreme situation of the small percentage (5 per cent) of pupils from a completely unilingual home environment who receive their instruction through the medium of their second language. We shall now turn to the more general question of comparing the scholastic achievements of pupils in unilingual (i.e. separate) medium schools and in bilingual (i.e. parallel and/or dual) medium schools.

These two questions are, however, related in a partial way. One of the objections advanced against the bilingual school is that, in its dual-medium form, it implies the use of the second language as a medium in teaching a certain proportion of content subjects—in other words, using the "wrong" medium with consequent retardation in the child's progress in those subjects. If, however, as has been shown above, in the South African situation this handicap is smaller than has been imagined, and is only of a temporary nature, then this objection to the dual-medium system practically falls away. The objection has even less force if it is remembered that we applied the crucial test to children with completely unilingual home environment. This was the most extreme case possible. Actually, as shown in Chapter V, our schools consist of a large proportion of pupils whose home and general environment is not completely unilingual, and in whose case the handicaps, due to use of the second language as medium, become proportionately less and less according to the degree in which the pupils have come into contact with the second language.

The above results present, however, merely *indirect* evidence on the pedagogical implications of the dual-medium form of the bilingual school. Let us now take the *direct* evidence by examining the results in the bilingual school itself. For the proof of the pudding is, after all, in the eating.

COMPARISON AT DIFFERENT INTELLIGENCE LEVELS. In this connection we shall bring in still another factor, the intelligence level of the pupils concerned. The contention is often made that while the partial use of the second language as a medium may have little or no deleterious effect on the learning process of children at the higher intelligence levels, it may prove a serious handicap in the case of pupils below average intelligence.

In order to answer this question we divided the pupils into four groups according to their Intelligence Quotients: A (I.Q. above 115),

B (I.Q. 100–115), C (I.Q. 85–100) and D (I.Q. below 85). A and B are above average and C and D below average. (100 I.Q. is the average.) These groupings were based on the results obtained from (1) the South African Group Test of Intelligence, which was given to all pupils; (2) the Beta test which is non-linguistic and which was given to the primary classes only; and (3) the Otis Advanced Intelligence Test, which was given to the high school classes only. In order to simplify the presentation of the results, we have for convenience combined these four into two main groups:

(1) Those above average intelligence (i.e. A and B) and
(2) Those below average intelligence (i.e. C and D).

The comparison between unilingual and bilingual schools can be made in respect of several different groups—according to *home language environment* (i.e. whether (i) mainly English, or (ii) mainly Afrikaans, or (iii) more or less bilingual; see page 46 above) and also according to the predominant *school medium*—English, or Afrikaans, or both. In a bilingual school, moreover, the children may be taught with their home language as medium in parallel groups in certain (usually the lower) classes, or they may have some of their subjects taught through one medium and others through the other medium in other (usually the higher) classes. Lastly, there are city schools, town schools and rural schools. In each type the organization as regards medium varies. There are also great differences between schools in the calibre of language teaching and in the "adjuvants" which aid language growth. And in many town and city schools, the children in the upper classes come from other parts and are the products of different types of schools. There are, therefore, many complicating factors which necessitate numerous subdivisions of the data. These have been analysed into hundreds of detailed tables and graphs.

Owing to limitations of space it is not possible to present here the details for all these sub-groups, nor for every individual standard separately, and we shall therefore have to limit ourselves to giving only the total averages, which indicate the main central tendencies, keeping constant in each case the most potent factors such as intelligence, home language and socio-economic environment. In view of the fact that of late there has been a good deal spoken from public platforms and written in the press about the detrimental educational consequences which are alleged to overtake the Afrikaans-speaking child if he is not taught in a unilingual Afrikaans medium school, the data which follow will have fuller information about this group than about the others. In order to narrow down the number of variable factors, the comparison between the unilingual and the bilingual type of school will be made within one homogeneous group, that of the 4,736 children with unilingual Afrikaans home environment (i.e. group (*a*) of Table on p. 46 above).

In other words, we are now comparing the scholastic achievement of *Afrikaans* children in unilingual Afrikaans medium schools with that of *Afrikaans* children in bilingual medium schools. The children were so selected that the average intelligence of these two groups of pupils was the same.

The comparison will be in respect of the two sets of scholastic data:

(*a*) Attainment in the two languages (English and Afrikaans).

(*b*) Attainment in content subjects (e.g. arithmetic and geography).

(*A*) LANGUAGE ATTAINMENT (ENGLISH AND AFRIKAANS)

The language tests used here were (*a*) Vocabulary, (*b*) Same-Opposites, (*c*) Story Completion, and (*d*) Speed and Comprehension of Reading. Parallel and equivalent sets of these tests were standardized for English and Afrikaans respectively. The results were combined into a weighted average of "standard" scores in each language. It has been found in previous investigations that the results of these four tests combined correlate highly with ability to use the language as a mode of expression, e.g. in composition both written and oral. As has been pointed out above (page 43), these tests are much more reliable measures of language ability than the ordinary school examinations. They have besides a range which makes objective comparisons of the absolute as well as the relative achievements between lower and higher classes possible. Finally the "standard" scores in the two languages are as nearly comparable as one can make them, e.g. a standard score of 500 in English or Afrikaans designates the same linguistic ability in each. (The language results given in the previous section were also derived from these tests.)

CHILDREN WITH PURELY AFRIKAANS HOME LANGUAGE. The following table and the accompanying graph show incidentally how extremely important the intelligence factor is in language achievement. The main point, however, is that the figures show a clear advantage in favour of the bilingual school as regards language attainment in both English and Afrikaans at all intelligence levels. We are dealing here with two controlled groups, and the gains though seemingly small are all statistically significant. To give some idea of the extent of this gain it may be mentioned that a gain of 20 represents about one-third of a year's linguistic growth per standard in each language.

The scores given are the averages for all standards combined from IV to X inclusive. As regards the individual standards, it may be mentioned that a consistent and considerable superiority in favour of the bilingual school over the unilingual school is registered in each of Standards IV, V, VI, VII and VIII. In Standards IX and X the unilingual school is slightly superior. This exception can be accounted

TABLE SHOWING COMPARISON OF LANGUAGE SCORES OF CHILDREN WITH
PURELY AFRIKAANS HOME LANGUAGE IN UNILINGUAL AND BILINGUAL
SCHOOLS RESPECTIVELY

(*a*) English Language Scores (Averages).

Intelligence Levels	In Unilingual (or separate) Medium Schools	In Bilingual (i.e. Parallel or Dual) Medium Schools
(i) Above average intelligence	442	459 (gain 17)
(ii) Below average intelligence	349	379 (gain 30)
Total	412	432 (gain 20)

(*b*) Afrikaans Language Scores (Averages)

(i) Above average intelligence	577	597 (gain 20)
(ii) Below average intelligence	497	519 (gain 22)
Total	550	570 (gain 20)

(*c*) Combined English and Afrikaans Scores (Averages)

(i) Above average intelligence	1,019	1,056 (gain 37)
(ii) Below average intelligence	846	898 (gain 52)
Total	962	1,002 (gain 40)

for by selective factors affecting adversely some of the bilingual schools in the smaller towns whence some of their brighter pupils migrate to the larger city unilingual schools for study beyond the Junior Certificate level. The intelligence scores in these two standards were slightly higher in the unilingual than in the bilingual school. The most significant result, however, is that the *greatest gain for the bilingual school is registered in the case of the lower intelligence groups.* Not only have they held more than their own in their first language, Afrikaans, but in their second language (English) their gain has been nearly twice as big as that registered by the higher intelligence group.

To sum up: Contrary to a general expectation, children with low intelligence have a relatively much better chance of becoming bilingual citizens (without loss in their mother tongue or in their content subjects

GRAPH V

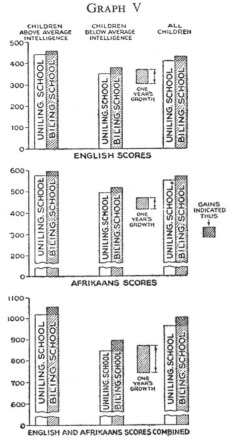

Graph comparing the attainment in LANGUAGES by Afrikaans home-language pupils in unilingual and bilingual schools respectively. Note how the bilingual school pupils do consistently better, *even in their mother tongue*, no matter whether they are: (*a*) above the average in intelligence, (*b*) below average, or (*c*) just normal, average children. In the comparison between the two types of school, home-language background has been kept constant.

—this latter point will be proved later) by attending the bilingual school than by attending the unilingual school. In other words, low intelligences derive a relatively greater linguistic gain by being in a bilingual school than high intelligences.

This gain is registered in spite of the fact that in the bilingual school these Afrikaans children received their instruction in the lower classes almost exclusively through the Afrikaans medium by means of the parallel class system and that it was generally only after Standard IV that English was also used as a medium in certain subjects under the dual-medium system.[1] The gain in the primary stages must be ascribed therefore to the association of Afrikaans and English-speaking children outside the classroom, on the playground and in the common exercises of the general assembly, etc. That this association is real and considerable is borne out by the following results based on the questionnaire given to each pupil tested, to ascertain the extent to which the second language was spoken in the playground. The questions put to the pupil in an English medium class were:

"Do you hear AFRIKAANS in the school playground?"
Underline (1) Always. (2) Often. (3) Sometimes. (4) Never.
"Do you speak AFRIKAANS in the school playground?"
Underline (1) Always. (2) Often. (3) Sometimes. (4) Never.

The pupil in an Afrikaans medium class had to answer similar questions in respect of ENGLISH. The system of scoring the responses is similar to that described in Chapter IV on the determination of the child's home language. The following ratings have been worked out on a 10-point scale for different types of schools.

Type of School	Frequency of Second Language Spoken and Heard in Playground
City unilingual Afrikaans medium	1·8
City unilingual English medium	2·5
Town Afrikans medium	3·3
Town English medium	3·4
English medium in parallel class school ...	7·1
Afrikaans medium in parallel class school ...	7·7

From the above results it is clear that the opportunities for actually using the second language outside the classroom (in the playground) are far greater in the case of the parallel class form of bilingual school where both sections meet each other than in the unilingual medium schools where the two sections are segregated more or less completely. In the town schools one still finds a certain amount of inevitable association because there, owing to circumstances, children are not so completely isolated by separate institutions as in the large unilingual city schools. The difference is noticeable in the above results.

CHILDREN WITH PURELY ENGLISH HOME LANGUAGE. If one compares the attainments in unilingual and bilingual schools respectively in regard to the converse situation, viz. the achievement of pupils from

[1] Where the dual-medium system was started a little earlier the gains in the second language scores were still more marked.

unilingual English-speaking homes who receive their instruction dominantly or exclusively in English medium classes, one finds that the gain in Afrikaans by those who attend the bilingual school over those in the unilingual (English medium) school is more than four times as great as the gain in English by Afrikaans pupils mentioned above. (The actual Afrikaans scores are 457 for bilingual school pupils as compared with 365 for unilingual school pupils: gain = 92.) Their attainment in English was practically not affected (577 for the unilingual and 574 for the bilingual school, the difference being statistically nonsignificant). The relative gains are illustrated in Graph VII, page 72.

The reasons for this much greater relative gain in bilingualism which accrues to the English pupil by virtue of his attending the bilingual school are probably: (a) the child with English home language is, to start with, on the whole less bilingual than the child with Afrikaans home language.[1] The former has therefore more leeway to make up. (b) Afrikaans is easier to learn than English with equal school and environmental opportunities.

In any case, the conclusion is clear, viz. that the English-speaking child to-day stands to gain more in bilingualism from attending a bilingual school than the Afrikaans-speaking child, and that by the more general adoption of the dual-medium principle in English schools the relative backwardness which the English-speaking section has thus far had in respect of bilingualism will be wiped out. Thereby that section will not only be able to compete more equally with the Afrikaans-speaking section, e.g. in the Public Service, but will also be enabled more fully to participate in South African life and citizenship than they are doing to-day.

CHILDREN WITH BILINGUAL HOME ENVIRONMENT. In the two previous

---

[1] This is evident also from the data given in previous sections. The fact that among the adult Afrikaners there have been many more cases of high-grade bilingualism than among the English-speaking South Africans can historically be accounted for by the fact that for several generations most of those with Afrikaans as home language received their schooling through the medium of English. *The Bilingual Quotients* of Afrikaans medium pupils are much higher than those of English medium pupils. This quotient represents the ratio of the pupil's score in his second language to that in his first language, expressed as a percentage.

Standard.				Afrikaans medium Pupils.	English medium Pupils.
IV	..	..	..	..	67·5	58·8
V	..	..	..	..	70·0	63·8
VI	..	..	..	..	73·5	67·9
VII	..	..	..	..	74·0	68·3
VIII	..	..	..	..	77·4	72·8
IX	..	..	..	..	84·8	76·5
X	..	..	..	..	87·4	80·1
No. of Cases	..	..	..	(3,052)	(3,473)

sections we have dealt with two homogeneous groups : (a) children with unilingual Afrikaans home background and (b) children with unilingual English home background ; i.e. the two extremes of the home language spectrum. We come now to the middle group, i.e. those children who have a more or less bilingual home background. It was essential for our investigation to keep this group separate and also to leave out the intermediate groups between the extreme unilingual groups and the central bilingual group. (See Table, p. 46 above.) Their inclusion with either of the extreme groups in this comparison would have vitiated our results, because one would then have been liable to ascribe to the school some of the achievement in bilingualism which was really due to the child's home environment.

The results would have been further complicated owing to the fact that children from more or less bilingual homes are on an average more intelligent than children from purely unilingual homes, whether English or Afrikaans. (This is borne out by the results of the Beta, Otis and South African group intelligence tests.) It might also be mentioned that children from bilingual homes who attend English medium schools have a higher average intelligence than bilingual children who go to Afrikaans medium schools. The difference on an average is about one-third of a year in mental growth for all standards. In the primary standards, however, according to the Beta test (which is an entirely non-linguistic measure of intelligence) the bilingual children in English medium are about three-fourths of a year ahead in mental growth of bilingual children in Afrikaans medium.

It is also found on the whole that bilingual children reach a higher all-round level of scholastic achievement than unilingual children. This superiority in intellectual development of bilingual over unilingual children is probably due largely to selective factors of a social nature which operate in South African society. The exact role which such factors play in South Africa must still be investigated. In any case, the conclusion arrived at by Arsenian as the result of the most exhaustive study made to date still stands : "No reliable differences in intelligence or age-grade status were disclosed between a group of monoglot and a group of bilingual children, matched person per person on race, sex, socio-economic status, and age in months." (*Bilingualism and Mental Development*, p. 153.)

In order to summarize the language attainments of the various groups discussed above, we give in the following table the average scores in English and Afrikaans language tests by these groups, according to their home language (i.e. unilingual English, unilingual Afrikaans and bilingual respectively) and the type and medium of school attended. By English medium and Afrikaans medium schools are meant *unilingual* medium schools. By bilingual school is meant a school where both media are used in varying proportions and includes the parallel class system in the elementary standards. We had to distinguish between two types of bilingual school, (a) where Afrikaans is predominant and (b) where English is predominant as a medium in the classes, because of the potent influence which even the partial use of a language as medium has upon the attainment in that language. In this table the results for city, town and rural schools are combined. The scores are the average "standard" scores for Standards IV to X inclusive.

SUMMARY TABLE

Comparative Attainment in Languages (English and Afrikaans)

Home Language and Medium of School	Average "Standard" Scores		
	In English	In Afrikaans	Total
Bilinguals in bilingual school with:			
(a) Predominantly English medium	570 ⎫	520 ⎫	1,090 ⎫
(b) Predominantly Afrikaans medium	430 ⎬ 500	580 ⎬ 550	1,010 ⎬ 1,050
Bilinguals in English medium school	565	490	1,055
Bilinguals in Afrikaans medium school	465	570	1,035
Unilingual Afrikaans children in English medium school ..	519	533	1,052
Unilingual Afrikaans children in bilingual school	432	570	1,002
Unilingual Afrikaans children in Afrikaans medium school	412	550	962
Unilingual English children in bilingual school	574	457	1,031
Unilingual English children in English medium school ..	577	365	942
Unilingual English children in Afrikaans medium school ..	(Not enough data for this group)		

CONCLUSIONS. It is very difficult in South Africa, where linguistic environments are so intertwined, to separate entirely the effects of school environment from those of the home and street environment; and, as we pointed out before, there is often the risk of ascribing to the

GRAPH VI

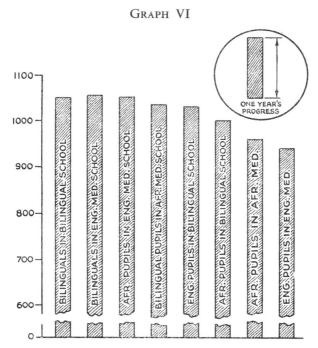

Graph showing the degree of bilingualism reached in different types of schools by pupils with different home backgrounds. Note how the lowest bilingualism is found where unilingual pupils attend unilingual schools.

former results which are really mainly due to the latter type of influence. Nevertheless we have tried by analysis in the accompanying table to group our data in such a way that the following conclusions may be drawn.[1]

(1) If one combines the scores in English and Afrikaans as an indication of bilingualism, those children with a bilingual home background who attend the bilingual medium school top the list, while right at the bottom of the list come the children with a unilingual home environment (English or Afrikaans) who attend a unilingual medium school (English or Afrikaans respectively.)

These are the two extremes where school and home pull in the same direction, reinforcing the advantages on the one hand and the handicaps on the other. There is no doubt that the child with a bilingual home and street environment has a great pull over the child with a unilingual environment. (See page 104, Chapter XI.)

(2) But even in the case of unilingual children the bilingual school

---

[1] See also Graph VI above.

achieves a higher attainment in the two languages combined than the unilingual school, whether English or Afrikaans medium. Unilingual English and Afrikaans home language children attending the bilingual medium school score 1,031 and 1,002, as compared with 942 and 962 respectively in the single medium schools. This is for the two languages combined.

(3) It is often maintained by those who attack the bilingual school that whatever may be the gains in the second language the child suffers in his mother tongue by attending the bilingual school. This is not borne out by the facts. On the contrary, if one takes the score in Afrikaans attained by the unilingual Afrikaans child attending the bilingual school and compares it with the score of the unilingual Afrikaans child attending the unilingual Afrikaans medium school, and similarly, if one compares the unilingual English child's achievements in English in a bilingual school with that in the unilingual English medium school, one can definitely conclude that the bilingual school offers no handicap in the study of the mother tongue.

These, be it noted, are conclusions in respect of children with unilingual home backgrounds. In the case of children with bilingual home environments there is no indication of their having suffered linguistically by attending the bilingual school. The relatively high combined score by the bilingual home environment children who attend the English medium school is partly due to the fact, mentioned above, that their average intelligence is relatively high compared with that of the other groups.

These are the main conclusions. There are many other interesting points, a few of which may be noted incidentally.

(4) As shown before, the potency of the use of the second language as a medium in furthering bilingualism is again demonstrated by the relatively high combined score (1,052) attained by Afrikaans children attending English medium schools.

(5) From the figures it would seem that if, quite apart from fostering bilingualism, one wanted to enhance the standard of Afrikaans by itself and of English by itself throughout the whole school population, the bilingual school offers the best facilities.

In order to present the argument in its simplest form, the results are presented on the next page in respect only of children with purely unilingual home environments in English and Afrikaans respectively. The least that one can claim from these results is that English as a subject by itself definitely does not suffer, and that Afrikaans is very considerably enhanced by the bilingual medium school organization, even when dealing with children with completely unilingual home environments.

(6) In drawing our conclusions from the figures in the following table, it must be noted that these figures are averages for groups summing up

Children with	English Scores		Afrikaans Scores	
	In Unilingual Schools	In Bilingual Schools	In Unilingual Schools	In Bilingual Schools
Unilingual Afrikaans home environment	412	432 (gain 20)	550	570 (gain 20)
Unilingual English home environment	577	574 (difference non-significant)	365	457 (gain 92)
Total	989	1,006 (gain 17)	915	1,027 (gain 112)

the scores of individuals who vary considerably in attainment within each group. These groups of schools include small rural and town schools as well as large city schools. Though the number of cases runs into thousands, the variation is considerable. Each average is therefore liable to a certain "probable error," which makes it risky to draw conclusions about differences smaller than 4 "standard" score points between these averages on the whole. Such small differences are statistically non-significant. For example, it will not be correct to conclude from the figures above that unilingual English-speaking children attending a bilingual school are necessarily inferior in English with a score of 574 to unilingual English pupils attending a unilingual school with a score of 577 in English.

An advance of 62 points on the standard score scale signifies one school year's growth on an average in the first language and 66 represents a school year's growth in the second language.

Thus it will be seen that Afrikaans children in unilingual Afrikaans medium schools are about two and a half years behind in English, compared standard for standard with English children in unilingual English medium schools. Similarly, English children in unilingual English medium schools are about three years behind in Afrikaans when compared standard for standard with Afrikaans children in unilingual Afrikaans medium schools.[1] This disparity is considerably lessened where these unilingual children attend bilingual schools. In Afrikaans, the disparity is reduced by more than a year and in English

[1] This is the only objective measure obtained thus far to show the actual difference, measured in terms of school years, between the standards in first and second languages represented by the A and B grades respectively in the Junior Certificate and Matriculation public examinations.

GRAPH VII

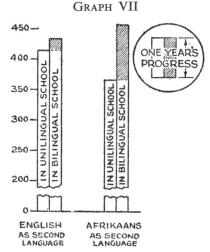

Graph showing superiority of second language attainments in the bilingual school by Afrikaans and English home language pupils. Note the great gain in Afrikaans by the English home language pupils in the bilingual school. This gain is far greater than that which the Afrikaans pupils gain in English by attending the bilingual school.

by about one-third of a year. This corroborates our previous finding that it is in teaching the unilingual English children more Afrikaans that the bilingual schools can make the biggest contribution. In other words, it is the unilingual English child who stands to gain most in bilingualism by attending the bilingual school.

(B) ATTAINMENT IN CONTENT SUBJECTS

Having now compared the bilingual school and the unilingual school with regard to the *language* attainments of their respective pupils, let us next compare them with regard to attainment in *content subjects*. In this comparison we shall confine ourselves to two representative school subjects, arithmetic and geography. The tests used in arithmetic, particularly on the mechanical side, involve the use of language to a lesser degree than those used in geography. The former are the same tests as were used in testing schools on the Carnegie Poor White Survey, and have well standardized forms both for the mechanical operations and the problems. The latter test has two equivalent forms each consisting of 50 items, covering the South African school syllabus fairly thoroughly.

The scores of these tests were reduced to "standard" scores which ensure equality of units all along the scale, both in geography and arithmetic. This enables the scores in these two subjects to be added together. In geography the pupils in the bilingual school were, on an average, about *four-fifths* of a school year ahead of those in the unilingual school. In arithmetic they were *half a year* ahead.

GRAPH VIII

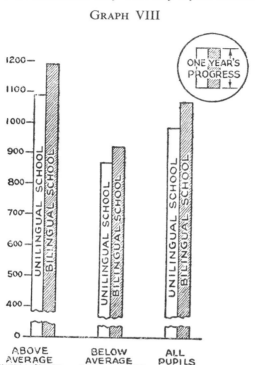

Graph comparing the attainments in CONTENT SUBJECTS by pupils in unilingual and bilingual schools respectively. Note how the bilingual school pupils do consistently better, no matter whether they are: (*a*) above the average in intelligence, (*b*) below average, or (*c*) just normal, average children. In the comparison between the two types of school home language background has been kept constant.

Comparing the pupils at different levels of intelligence: (i) those below average intelligence and (ii) those above average intelligence, we have the total results of Arithmetic and Geography combined as shown in Graph VIII. The superiority of the bilingual school pupils at both levels of intelligence is clearly seen. Though these average results are each subject to a certain probable error (owing to the fact that we are dealing only with a sample of the total school population of South Africa) the differences between the two types of schools are all statistically significant. The superiority of the bilingual school is found consistently in all standards from IV to X inclusive.

It must be remembered (as was pointed out above) that there is no significant difference between the *average* intelligence of the pupils in the two types of school here compared. Though the intelligence in Standards IX and X of the bilingual school is slightly lower owing to selection, as was mentioned above, the superiority of the bilingual school is probably due to more efficient instruction and richer learning experiences in that type of school as compared with the unilingual school. It may be that the bilingual school attracts the better type of teacher on the whole—viz. the thoroughly bilingual teacher. If present-day tendencies in the selection and training of teachers however continue, we have reason to fear that this type of teacher will slowly be dying out. This by the way. A more detailed analysis of the underlying factors must still be made before we can say definitely how much of the result is due to this or to that specific cause. For the present our main purpose has been merely to record this phenomenon as a fact in our South African schools.

The second important point on which these results throw light for the first time in South African educational research, as far as I know it, is the position of the child below average intelligence who is taught partly on the dual-medium system. Here we can now definitely say that he does not suffer in the least in arithmetic or in geography. On the contrary, he registers beyond Standard IV significant gains in both these subjects over his fellows who are taught in the unilingual school.

The above results are in respect of children with unilingual home environment. As for children with bilingual home environment, here too we find that these children do better in the bilingual school than in the unilingual school, probably because in the former type of school their whole linguistic experience is made use of in the learning process and not merely half or a third of it, as inevitably happens when these bilingual home language children are forced into a single medium school. As has been pointed out before, our results in the content subjects show a marked superiority in scholastic attainment on the part of the children with bilingual home environment over those with unilingual home environment, whether English or Afrikaans.

CHAPTER VIII

SOCIAL ATTITUDES IN BILINGUAL AND UNILINGUAL SCHOOLS

THE next question to consider is how children of bilingual schools compare with those of unilingual schools with regard to their respective attitudes towards the other section as well as towards the cultural matters and institutions usually associated with the other language and those who speak it. In other words, do English and Afrikaans-speaking children become more tolerant towards each other, and do they show a greater appreciation of each other's language and point of view by being taught together in one school instead of in separate schools? Assuming that children come to school with certain prejudices which they inevitably bring from their homes, does the school serve to break these down, or to intensify them? It is assumed in this study that situations which eradicate feelings of hostile discrimination and antagonism between the two sections, with a view to fusing the Europeans in South Africa into one united nation, are desirable. There is, however, an appreciable body of people in this country who would not accept this assumption. For them any idea of fusion is repugnant. According to their point of view situations which tend to eradicate these sectional prejudices are undesirable. They maintain that the two sections must at all costs be kept "pure." To prevent mixing there must be separate institutions or spheres of operation all along the line. Like parallel lines the two should never meet, except perhaps in heaven.

The acceptance or non-acceptance of these assumptions is, however, a matter of argument and opinion, depending upon one's social and political philosophy about South Africa's future. It is not proposed to discuss the pros and cons of the argument here. We want to show rather what actually does happen in our schools. In other words we are concerned here only with the *facts*.

In order to get an objective measure of the prevailing attitudes amongst our schoolchildren, we casually interspersed certain attitude questions amongst the series of purely informational questions regarding their age, standard, occupation of father, names of books, newspapers and magazines read in the home, church denomination, names of towns visited, etc. These questions were designed to elicit their attitude towards English and Afrikaans as school subjects and wireless media, and towards institutions like the Boy Scouts, Girl Guides and Voortrekkers, or "God Save the King" and "Die Stem." They had also to name who in their opinion were South Africa's greatest statesmen or national leaders, artists, etc.

F   75

There were questions such as the following:

(i) Do you think that English-speaking and Afrikaans-speaking children should go to the same or to different schools? (Write *same* or *different*.)

(ii) Do you think that English-speaking and Afrikaans-speaking children should play in the same or different teams in sport? (Write *same* or *different*.)

(iii) A team from a neighbouring town is coming to play against your school. They have to remain overnight. The principal has asked you to find out if your parents are willing to put up some of the children. All you know about the boys is their names, which are as follows: Piet Wessels, Bob Andrews, Jock McGavin, Koos Swanepoel, Willie van Rooyen, Tom Armstrong, Harry Parker, Jannie van der Merwe, Attie van der Walt, Maxwell Prentice, Jack Evans, and Fanie Coetzee. Supposing it is possible for your parents to accommodate *two* of the boys at your house, which two would you choose? (Underline their names.)

After the whole test had been completed the pupils were asked to go back to these questions and to write down on the lines provided below each the *reason* for that particular response. This procedure was adopted because of the tendency of children to give a response for which they can supply the most plausible reason. Now, however, they had committed themselves and were told not to alter their choices when giving their reasons. The whole test was marked "Confidential," and it was stressed that neither their teachers nor anyone known to them would see their answers. They should therefore give their opinions honestly and frankly.

Quite apart from the responses themselves, the *reasons* afforded the best insight into the children's attitudes which were sometimes quite unconsciously expressed. For example, in the choice of the names of boys in the last question many gave quite rational responses, e.g. "We speak only Afrikaans at home and therefore I underlined boys with Afrikaans names, as they would feel more at home." The same with English. "We hear so little Afrikaans in our home and I thought it would give me a chance to practise my Afrikaans, so I underlined two Afrikaans boys." The height of reasonableness and absence of discrimination was reached in responses of the following kind: "I underlined an English name and an Afrikaans name, as they would be equally welcome in our home."

On the other hand there were responses which showed definite discrimination of a more or less adverse kind, e.g. "I underlined two English names because they are English and therefore decent!" Or, "Ons wil g'n verdomde Engelse in ons huis hê nie."

The responses to this particular question were classified into three categories according as they were (a) sympathetic, (b) neutral and (c) adversely discriminatory towards the other section. In the neutral category were placed, among others, the playful and utterly irrelevant reasons which sometimes occurred. For example: "Maxwell Prentice sounds to me like a pansy boy. I'd rather have Attie van der Walt, who sounds like a real sport." "Fanie Coetzee is my neef." (This upon investigation turned out to be a fact.) "Hulle het dalk mooi susters!" and so on. While a certain amount of playfulness is to be expected wherever children are concerned, it is significant that this type of irrelevancy and lightheartedness occurred more frequently in those groups of children with whom there was little or no evidence of conscious animus, dislike or contempt in their attitude to the other section.

In the unilingual schools the pupils registered a much higher degree of adverse discrimination than in the bilingual schools, the highest being in the Afrikaans single medium schools. This is however the result of only one single question. In order to get a more reliable index of the children's social attitudes, we combined the results of all the attitude tests mentioned above. It must be remembered that these results represent the view of over 18,000 pupils from Standards IV to X (inclusive) from all types of homes and schools. We finally classified the responses to all the questions into four categories according as they displayed *sectional discrimination*[1]: (a) None, (b) Slight, (c) Decided and (d) Excessive.

It is interesting to compare the frequency with which excessive dislike or contempt occurred in the responses of pupils in unilingual Afrikaans medium, unilingual English medium and bilingual medium schools respectively. 10·7 per cent of the responses in the unilingual Afrikaans medium schools in the large cities showed *excessive* discrimination, compared with 2·0 per cent in the unilingual English medium city schools. Town English medium schools showed 1·7 per cent, while Town Afrikaans medium schools showed only 2·2 per cent excessive discrimination. Dual and parallel medium schools registered 2·7 per cent and Rural Afrikaans schools 3·7 per cent. So much for the (d) "Excessive" category.

A better all-round index of strong discrimination is, however, obtained by combining the (c) "decided" and (d) "excessive" groups. The total results are given in the following table:

---

[1] I prefer to use the term "sectional" discrimination, for want of a better term, rather than the one more commonly used in South Africa, viz. "racial" discrimination. In the accepted sense of the term *race*, as it is used in the anthropological and sociological sciences, I do not think it is correct to speak of *racial* differences when we refer to the cultural differences between the Afrikaans and English sections of the European population in South Africa. It would seem more correct for us in South Africa to reserve the use of the term *racial* to the differences between black and white in our country.

Type of School	Percentage of Pupils Showing Strong Sectional Discrimination
Unilingual (City) Afrikaans Medium ..	50 ⎫ 37
Unilingual (Town) Afrikaans medium	27 ⎭
Unilingual (City) English medium ..	16 ⎫ 17
Unilingual (Town) English medium ..	19 ⎭
Rural Afrikaans medium	38
Bilingual medium (parallel and dual) English dominant	20
Bilingual medium (parallel and dual) Afrikaans dominant	20

There is no significant difference between the two types of bilingual school organization, parallel class or dual-medium, in the degree of discrimination. If anything, there is a slight difference in favour of the dual-medium types. Because these differences are so small we have grouped the two together.

The relatively high degree of sectional discrimination shown by the pupils of the unilingual City Afrikaans medium school in comparison with Town Afrikaans medium on the one hand and City English medium on the other hand, may be attributed partly to the fact that the Afrikaans-speaking group is usually in the minority in the cities and consequently would tend to be on the defensive and to display inferiority reactions towards the English-speaking majority in the large city.

The English-speaking group in the large city, on the other hand, is not so solicitous (at least not to the same extent as the Afrikaans minority) over their language or cultural distinctiveness. They tacitly assume that they are superior in other ways as well as numerically. Considering themselves in an unassailable position culturally, they can afford to be tolerant, if not patronizing, to the Afrikaans minority group.

This attitude is revealed in the unconsciously naïve responses of the children which as a rule reflect fairly faithfully the social attitude found in the home or deliberately engendered in the school. For example, in giving their reasons for preferring to have Afrikaans-speaking children in the same school with English-speaking children rather than in separate schools, children of the Natal English-speaking majority group tend to be patronizing on general humanitarian grounds towards Afrikaans children: "Afrikaans children are also human beings." "They are also white people." "They might feel hurt if they were sent to different schools." And so these responses display discrimination by unconscious innuendo in varying degrees which can be graded on a scale in descending order till we come to ones that are simply and rationally tolerant like: "They are as nice as we are." "There is no difference between us except languages, and that does not matter as we are all South Africans." "We have a lot to learn from each other."

Still, this small-minority-complex theory does not altogether account for the fact that there should be such a high degree of racial discrimination in the unilingual (Afrikaans) medium schools of Pretoria, 65 per cent (25 per cent excessive), where the English and Afrikaans-speaking groups are socially and economically as well as numerically not far apart on an average. Nor does it provide an adequate reason for the fact that a large Afrikaans-medium high school in Cape Town registered over 70 per cent strong anti-English discrimination (26 per cent excessive) which is the highest of all the large schools tested in the country. That school is attended on an average by children from a well-established and in no way socially or culturally inferior Afrikaans community at the Cape.

Whatever the reasons may be (and here we get into the realm of theory and opinion), the main fact that stands out in the above figure is the relatively low index of sectional discrimination (20 per cent) registered in the bilingual school in comparison with the unilingual school, particularly on the Afrikaans side (50 per cent). This fact disposes in a definite way of the theory often advanced in categorical terms by advocates of the unilingual school, that if one mixes the two sections in one school one aggravates the antipathies which these children bring from their homes, and that it is far better to keep them in separate schools where each section will find itself and will in consequence respect and appreciate the other section better. Theories like these must be based on isolated but striking instances of antipathy which no doubt may have occurred in bilingual schools. We have here to do with the situation as a whole and to base our conclusions on the rule and not on the exceptions. We know that where these exceptions occurred they were frequently due to bad handling of the situation by a principal who was himself not free from strong prejudices and under whom the minority group in the bilingual school was placed in an invidious position of inferiority. These cases do exist. But the remedy is at hand. Train and appoint for such schools only bilingual principals with the widest sympathies towards both sections.

THE SAME OR SEPARATE SCHOOLS

Some interesting points emerge from the answers to the question: "Do you think that English-speaking and Afrikaans-speaking children should go to the *same* or *separate* schools?" The percentage preferring the *same* schools *increases* as the standards get higher from 27 per cent in Standard IV to 73 per cent in Standard X. This would seem to indicate that children as they progress in school become less prone to the isolationistic prejudices which they bring to school when they start.

This is the trend for all types of schools combined. There is an upward trend to a greater or less extent in all the different types of schools, with one exception, viz. in the unilingual (City) Afrikaans medium schools where the trend is in the opposite direction in the upper standards.

The total results are given in the accompanying table. These percentages give those who desire the *same* schools. 100 minus this percentage would of course give the percentage desiring *separate* schools.

TABLE SHOWING PERCENTAGES OF PUPILS IN EACH STANDARD CHOOSING THE SAME INSTEAD OF SEPARATE SCHOOLS FOR ENGLISH AND AFRIKAANS-SPEAKING CHILDREN

Type of School	IV	V	VI	VII	VIII	IX	X	Total
City Afrikaans unilingual medium	9	12	30	35	60	50	26	33
Rural Afrikaans medium	20	40	36	46	68	—	—	—
Town Afrikaans medium	27	27	32	70	77	83	69	49
Town English medium	21	32	33	75	79	89	95	49
City English unilingual medium	16	32	46	54	67	76	78	48
Bilingual (i.e. parallel and dual) with Afrikaans medium dominant	54	73	84	74	82	85	88	75
Bilingual (i.e. parallel and dual) with English medium dominant	44	50	66	70	65	75	82	62
Total	27	38	47	61	71	76	73	Total average 60 per cent

The following are some of the salient points to be noted in the accompanying table:

(1) The unilingual Afrikaans medium city schools which displayed the greatest degree of sectional discrimination also have the greatest percentage who view the association of English and Afrikaans-speaking children in the same schools with disfavour. Only 33 per cent expressed themselves in favour of the *same* school here, compared with about 50 per cent in the unilingual English medium schools and about 70 per cent in the bilingual medium school (75 per cent with Afrikaans and 62 per cent with English as dominant medium).

(2) In studying the trend of opinion with the advance in school one finds

that while the upward trend in the unilingual City Afrikaans medium school starts at Standard IV with only 9 per cent in favour of the same school (i.e. 91 per cent against) and ends with only 26 per cent at Standard X, the bilingual medium school (with dominant Afrikaans medium) begins with 54 per cent at Standard IV and goes up to 85 per cent in Standard VI and ends with 88 per cent in Standard X. In fact, the bilingual school stays on a plateau bordering on 80 per cent in the high school classes. Further, the unilingual city Afrikaans medium school, on the other hand, shows (as we mentioned above) a sharp decline from Standard VIII onwards, i.e. from about 60 per cent to about 26 per cent in Standard X. There is a decline also in the last two years in the unilingual Town Afrikaans medium school. In sharp contrast with this is the steady upward trend in the case of the unilingual English medium schools in the percentage of those who consider it desirable that English and Afrikaans-speaking children should attend the same schools—the Town English medium Standard X registering the highest figure of the lot, viz. 95 per cent.

(3) *Total result*: Taking all types of school together, we find that about 60 per cent chose the same school and 40 per cent chose different schools. This is a very significant majority of our children in favour of associating with the other section—in spite of the fact that the large majority of these children are actually in separate schools. So that it cannot be said that they were merely seeking to justify the situation in which they found themselves.

Lack of space prevents us from giving here the detailed statistics according to provinces. It may be noted as a point of interest, however, that the total average percentage for all types of pupils preferring the same school for the two sections is considerably higher in the Cape (75 per cent) than in the Transvaal (56 per cent) and in Natal (60 per cent). Can it be that this is a vestige or symptom of the Cape's greater reputed liberalism? Or is it merely the fact that the deliberate drive in recent years for separate schools had not yet penetrated to the Cape children to the same extent as in the Transvaal?

THE SAME OR SEPARATE SPORTS TEAMS

The responses to the question regarding sport: "Do you think that English and Afrikaans-speaking children should play in the same or different teams in sport?" revealed almost exactly the same relative differences between the different types of schools. But here the percentages for the same team were consistently bigger. Thus 74 per cent were for the same *team* while 26 per cent were against, compared with the 60/40 majority for the same *school*. The percentages for the Cape, Natal and Transvaal were 83, 79 and 70 respectively.

The total percentages for the different types of school were:

	Percentage Choosing the Same Team
Unilingual English medium school	90
Bilingual school	85
Unilingual Afrikaans medium school	55

EFFECT OF HOME LANGUAGE ON CHOICE

Besides dividing up the responses of the pupils according to the medium of the school and the school standards, we further divided them according to home language into three main groups: (a) home language more or less unilingual Afrikaans; (b) home language more or less unilingual English; (c) home language more or less bilingual. These three groups do not exhaust all the pupils tested, for we took out the intermediate groups on either side of the bilingual group (see Table on page 46 above) in order to arrive at more clear-cut results for groups (a), (b) and (c). The results are given in the following table:

Home Language	Percentage Choosing	
	Same School	Same Team
(a) Unilingual Afrikaans	57	65
(b) Unilingual English	60	80
(c) Bilingual	72	80
Total (average)	60	74

The Cape consistently had the highest percentages for all three home language groups, registering 69 per cent, 78 per cent and 76 per cent for groups (a), (b) and (c) respectively in preferring the same school and 76 per cent, 87 per cent and 83 per cent respectively for the same sports team. The Transvaal is consistently lower than the Cape even with the bilingual home language group. This group registered 68 per cent for the same school and 77 per cent for the same team, compared with the Cape's 76 per cent and 83 per cent respectively.

As can be expected in the light of the foregoing results, the highest percentages in favour of the same school and the same team are to be found in the case of children from bilingual homes attending bilingual schools. In fact as a group they reach and exceed the 90 per cent level. Here the school and the home work in the same direction.

The lowest degree of enthusiasm for the same school is found among children with unilingual Afrikaans home language attending a unilingual Afrikaans medium school. Here the school seems to accentuate the discriminatory prejudices of the home. The same intensification is found among children from unilingual English homes attending a unilingual English medium school, but nothing like to the same extent as with the former Afrikaans group.

Where the *child from a unilingual home goes to a bilingual school we find him on the whole much more ready to co-operate with the other section than the child who goes to the unilingual school.* In the bilingual school, the school seems to compensate for the isolationist tendencies brought from the home.

REASONS FOR CHOICE

Let us in conclusion look at the reasons the children gave for choosing the same or different school. One could write a whole dissertation on these. The reasons were cross classified also according to home language and type of school as well as according to standards.

The reasons stressing the language aspect were predominant. Those in favour of the same school stressed the fact that it promotes a knowledge of both official languages. Those against the same school held that one or both languages would suffer. In some English schools the fear was expressed that "the English accent might be affected." The fear that Afrikaans might swamp English was never expressed by an English child. The opposite fear that "English might oust Afrikaans" was sometimes found. Subconsciously a number of responses seemed to regard English as the stronger language.

The promotion of a knowledge of both languages was most frequently stressed amongst (a) children with bilingual home environment and (b) children attending parallel and dual-medium classes, and least frequently amongst the unilingual Afrikaans home children attending Afrikaans medium city and rural schools.

Solicitude about the dangers of the Afrikaner losing his language and "kultuur" by attending the same school with English-speaking children is most frequently found in the senior classes of the unilingual Afrikaans medium city and rural schools and not half as frequently in the town Afrikaans medium schools. Even in these schools the bilingual home language pupils do not express such fears in anything like the same proportion.

Reasons of a political nature are relatively rare among children, and the problems of an administrative nature which the school catering for both sections might offer are hardly mentioned at all. Wholly imaginary medium difficulties were mentioned by far the most often amongst Afrikaans home language pupils attending Afrikaans unilingual city schools. Why this group should be more ignorantly prejudiced than other groups as to even the most elementary facts regarding language and medium questions it is difficult to say except on the assumption that they have been deliberately misled by propaganda.

In conclusion, it may be mentioned that among the reasons given for preferring separate schools occurred expressions of dislike of, or contempt for, the other language or section which by their frequency afforded an index of the degree of invidious sectional discrimination present in each of the different types of school. Analysis of the results leads to the following conclusions:

(a) Adverse sectional discrimination is from three to four times as great in unilingual as in bilingual schools.
(b) Of the unilingual schools it is greater in the Afrikaans medium than in the English medium schools.
(c) Of the bilingual schools it is slightly greater in those where English is predominant than in those where Afrikaans is predominant.
(d) The children with bilingual home environment display the least adverse discrimination.

As to the reliability of the above data, it may be mentioned that these are based on about 18,000 responses and, as one gets beyond ten thousand cases, the percentages reflecting the various tendencies take on a rock-like steadiness which is never found where one works only with a few hundred cases. The multiplication of cases eliminates the chance variations due to selection and sampling and is the only true basis for generalization of any kind. The consistency of our data on the main issue leaves no doubt about the fact that in bilingual (i.e. the parallel and dual) medium schools, where pupils of both sections mix and associate freely, the children display a comparatively low degree of intercultural antagonism.

GRAPH IX

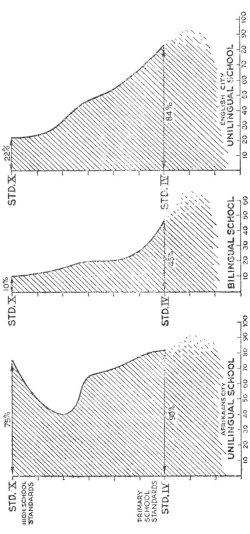

Graph showing in rough and schematic way the degree of "racial" discrimination present in schools of different types as indicated by the percentage of children who think that English and Afrikaans-speaking children should be kept in two separate camps. Children, when they start school, bring from their homes certain very decided "racial" prejudices which tend to diminish as they go up higher in the school standards. By the time they get to Standard IV there is a good deal of this feeling of separateness still present. In the unilingual school it still stands in the region of 80 per cent to 90 per cent, while in the bilingual school it has already dropped to 45 per cent. This is at the Standard IV stage, which is the point at which we started measuring their attitudes. The graph shows clearly what happens in the following standards in each of the three types of school. In the diagram on the right it shows how in the case of the English (city) unilingual school this feeling of separateness diminishes steadily as one goes upwards on to the high-school standards until it reaches a figure of 22 per cent in Standard X. Compare with this the diagram on the left, which depicts the situation in the Afrikaans (city) unilingual school. Here we find a slower decrease in the feeling as one goes up. But the most striking and curious phenomenon here is the revival of this feeling of separateness in the upper standards of the high school, culminating in the very large proportion of 75 per cent in Standard X. Contrast with this the relatively small degree of racial discrimination and the rapid tapering off in the upper classes of the bilingual school represented by the middle diagram. Here only 10 per cent of the matriculants leave school with those sentiments compared with 22 per cent in the unilingual English medium school and 75 per cent in the unilingual Afrikaans medium school.

CHAPTER IX

SOCIAL ATTITUDES AMONG NORMAL COLLEGE STUDENTS

ATTITUDE tests were given to the student-teachers of the four Normal Colleges in the Transvaal. Three of these are Afrikaans medium (Pretoria, Potchefstroom and Heidelberg) and one is English medium (Johannesburg).

THE SAME *VERSUS* SEPARATE SCHOOLS

The attitude of these student-teachers on the question of the desirability of pupils of the two cultural sections being educated in the same or in separate schools can be gauged from the following figures:

	Percentage Choosing	
	Same School	Separate Schools
Afrikaans medium Normal Colleges ..	67	33
English medium Normal Colleges ..	87	13
Total (average) ..	72	28

From the above it will be seen that nearly three-fourths of all students voted for the *same* school. Over 90 per cent of the students who were themselves taught through the English medium at school voted for the *same* school, compared with 66 per cent who had received their own schooling through Afrikaans medium. These are both very substantial majorities.

The three chief reasons advanced for advocating the same school were:

(a) Opportunity of becoming bilingual, as bilingualism is essential in South Africa.

(b) A mutual respect will be fostered by learning each other's point of view, customs, etc.

(c) It will eradicate "racialism."

The three most frequent reasons advanced in favour of separate schools were:

(a) A child progresses better in his own language.

(b) The philosophy of life of the two "nations" is different and separation will aid the process of character building.

86

(c) Separation will prevent friction and difficulties between the children of the two "nations."

On the whole, "political" reasons were much more frequent among these students than among the schoolchildren, probably because the former are more mature and have developed theories about South Africa's political future.

CLOSER ASSOCIATION OF TWO SECTIONS

We give next the students' opinions on two further questions:

(a) To what extent should there be co-operation and fusion of interests between the two sections of the white people in South Africa?
(b) Should teachers holding extreme political views be allowed to indoctrinate the children in their charge?

In order to measure their reactions on these two main questions, a test was presented to them as follows:

Below you will find a number of statements about which people may genuinely hold conflicting opinions. You are asked to read each statement carefully and then to mark it in the way you yourself actually feel and think. Be completely frank—your own responses will be regarded as confidential.

Indicate the amount of your agreement or disagreement by placing one of the following letters in the margin before each statement:

> A—strongly in agreement.
> B—in agreement.
> C—undecided or in doubt.
> D—in disagreement.
> E—strongly in disagreement.

Then following 20 statements. Some dealt with other questions, e.g. the Native question, immigration, etc. Since not all of the 20 are relevant to our present discussion we shall deal with the following ten only:

(1) The differences that divide the two dominant white "races" in South Africa are so great that any attempt at securing co-operation between them should be regarded as both undesirable and futile.
(2) As things are in South Africa to-day, all attempts at promoting co-operation on a national basis between the two dominant white "races" are premature and should not be supported.
(3) While admitting the desirability of some national ideal common to both the dominant white "races," every white South African should strive in the first place to realize the ideals of his own group.
(4) Intermarriage between members of the two dominant "races" in

South Africa is detrimental to the cultural development of the South African people.

(5) Every white South African who has the real interests of his country at heart should strive to bring about as complete an identity or fusion of interests as possible between the two dominant white "races."

(6) When all is said and done, close and friendly co-operation between the two dominant white "races" should remain the national ideal of every white South African.

(7) The best way to obtain bilingualism at school is to use the second language as medium in the case of at least half the school subjects as soon as the pupils can follow instruction in the second language.

(8) (*a*) Teachers in secondary schools who hold very extreme or revolutionary views should be allowed to discuss them freely with their students, provided that they do so in an objective way. (*b*) What about teachers in primary schools?

(9) School teachers who hold very extreme or revolutionary views should be warned to keep their mouths shut unless they wish to be dismissed.

(10) School teachers who hold very extreme or revolutionary views should be given complete freedom and even encouraged to engage in propaganda both inside as well as outside the school.

The percentages A, B, C, D and E for each of these questions were worked out for each normal college separately and for the lot combined. Lack of space prevents us from giving the detailed tables here. The following points of interest, however, may be mentioned. We shall deal first with the student body as a whole and then with those of the different institutions typifying reactions of English and Afrikaans medium students separately.

I. Reactions of All Students:

(i) The first six statements concern co-operation between the two white sections of the population.

(ii) The last three statements concern the degree to which teachers should influence pupils in their charge.

(iii) In order to increase the reliability of our total results there was some deliberate repetition, the same question being repeated in different forms, sometimes positively and sometimes negatively, but with a slight shade of difference.

(iv) Roughly two-thirds of these student-teachers agree that close and friendly co-operation between the two sections is an ideal to strive for. About a quarter believe the opposite. They hold that co-operation is futile and should not be sought.

(v) The question concerning the desirability of intermarriage reveals an interesting difference of opinion. Nearly a fifth take up a non-committal attitude. Those who are strongly opposed to inter-marriage are slightly more numerous than those strongly in favour. But those merely in favour outweigh those merely against. In general, therefore, we may conclude that students are fairly evenly divided on this rather fundamental question. As the question is framed it is impossible to say whether the reaction is based on emotional or on purely intellectual grounds.

(vi) The proposal to use one language as the medium for half the subjects and the other for the other half caused a very considerable split of opinion, as many being opposed as those in favour. One-fifth had no decided reaction.

(vii) About a third of the students believe that teachers should be permitted to discuss freely extreme or revolutionary views in *high* schools. About half oppose this view. The percentage who oppose the discussion of extreme views in primary schools is appreciably bigger.

(viii) Not quite half of the students were in favour of "muzzling" teachers.

(ix) Only about 10 per cent of students were in favour of school teachers being encouraged to make propaganda for their views inside as well as outside the school. Indeed, this question evoked the highest percentage of votes "strongly against" of all the questions considered above. It is noteworthy, too, that the percentage of "neutrals" was lower than in any other question. We return to this question later, as it touches on rather an important point in South African education.

II. REACTION OF STUDENTS IN DIFFERENT INSTITUTIONS. In order to compare the reactions of students in the four Normal Colleges of the Transvaal it will not be necessary for our present purpose to reproduce their reactions to all the ten questions reviewed above. Accordingly, we shall select Nos. 5 and 10 for comparison and discussion.

The following points may be noted in the accompanying table:

(i) A little over half of the students at Potchefstroom (53 per cent) and Heidelberg (58 per cent) expressed themselves as in favour of working for co-operation and a fusion of interests.

(ii) Heidelberg and Potchefstroom, however, also recorded the highest percentage as *strongly* opposed to this ideal—more than twice as many as at Pretoria and more than four times as many as at Johannesburg.

(iii) Johannesburg students were most wholehearted in supporting strongly the ideal of fusion of interests, 67 per cent being strongly in favour compared with Pretoria's 30 per cent, Potchefstroom's 26 per cent and Heidelberg's 22 per cent.

PERCENTAGE OF STUDENTS SIGNIFYING VARYING DEGREES OF AGREEMENT AND DISAGREEMENT WITH CERTAIN STATEMENTS

Statement	Institution	Agree Strongly (A)	Agree (B)	Undecided (C)	Disagree (D)	Disagree Strongly (E)	Unspecified	Total
5. Every white South African who has the real interests of his country at heart should strive to bring about as complete an identity or fusion of interests as possible between the two dominant white "races."	Potchefstroom	26	27	8	21	13	5	100
	Heidelberg	22	36	2	24	14	2	100
	Pretoria	30	41	7	14	36	2	100
	Johannesburg	67	20	9	1	3	—	100
10. School teachers who hold very extreme views should be given complete freedom and even encouraged to engage in propaganda both inside as well as outside the school.	Potchefstroom	13	8	5	26	40	8	100
	Heidelberg	6	10	8	46	30	—	100
	Pretoria	1	3	4	37	55	—	100
	Johannesburg	4	—	4	18	72	2	100

(iv) If we take the combined percentage who *disagree* and *strongly disagree* with this ideal, we have the institutions in the following order:

Johannesburg	.. 4
Pretoria ..	.. 20
Potchefstroom	.. 34
Heidelberg	.. 38

(v) In going over to the next statement we find that Potchefstroom showed the largest percentage *strongly* in favour of teachers making propaganda in the schools for their own views. If we combine the A's and B's, i.e. those who *strongly agree* with those who *agree* with this point of view, the institutions arrange themselves in the following order:

Johannesburg	.. 4
Pretoria ..	.. 4
Heidelberg	.. 16
Potchefstroom	.. 21

(vi) The most significant point in the above table is the clear indication that the larger the percentage of students who favour racial co-operation, the smaller the percentage who would use the schools for purposes of propaganda.

III. REACTION OF ENGLISH AND AFRIKAANS MEDIUM NORMAL COLLEGES COMPARED. In the accompanying table Pretoria, Heidelberg and

ATTITUDES OF ENGLISH AND AFRIKAANS MEDIUM NORMAL COLLEGES COMPARED

Statement (abbreviated)	Type of Institution	Agree strongly (A)	Agree (B)	Undecided (C)	Disagree (D)	Disagree strongly (E)	Unspecified	Total
No. 5. Promote fusion of interests between two sections	Afrikaans medium..	26	35	6	19	11	3	100
	English medium..	67	20	9	1	3	—	100
No. 10. Teachers to engage in political propaganda inside as well as outside the school	Afrikaans medium ..	7	6	5	36	43	3	100
	English medium..	4	—	4	18	72	2	100

G

Potchefstroom are grouped together as Afrikaans medium institutions and Johannesburg forms a class by itself as the only English medium institution.

The following points from the above table need emphasis:

(i) It is clear that the English medium institution has, relatively, considerably more student-teachers (87 per cent) in favour of striving to bring about real co-operation than the Afrikaans medium institutions (61 per cent). It should be stressed, however, that even in the Afrikaans institutions considerably more students are in favour of this ideal than are opposed to it.

(ii) The idea that teachers should make propaganda in schools is more strongly supported in the predominantly Afrikaans medium institutions than in the English. The English medium institution also shows a far higher percentage of students (72 per cent) *strongly* against the spreading of propaganda in the schools than the Afrikaans medium institutions (43 per cent).

(iii) It should be noted, however, that the percentage of students in Afrikaans medium institutions who favour the spreading of propaganda in schools is very considerably lower than the percentage who are opposed to sectional co-operation as outlined in the statement above (No. 5).

TO WHAT EXTENT DO STUDENTS WHO OPPOSE "RACIAL" OR SECTIONAL CO-OPERATION BELIEVE IN TEACHERS MAKING PROPAGANDA?

To answer this question more decisively than was possible by mere inspection of the above tables, two correlations were worked out for what are considered to be two fairly homogeneous, as well as representative groups:

(*a*) for Afrikaans-speaking students at Potchefstroom, and

(*b*) for English-speaking (3rd and 4th year) students at Johannesburg.

The method adopted was Pearson's corrective formula for broad grouping assuming normal distributions of the variates. In the case of the Afrikaans-speaking students a correlation of 0·57 plus, 0·009 minus, was obtained. For the English-speaking students no significant correlation was obtained. It is interesting to note that 38 out of the 76 final-year students considered voted *strongly* for racial co-operation and just as *strongly against* the use of propaganda in the schools.

Finally, we considered to what extent the students' attitudes on these questions were affected by the length of time they had been in training at these various institutions. Accordingly, separate percentages were worked out for the students in their second, third and fourth years. An inspection of these figures suggests that the length of training has no appreciable influence on the opinions of students. It may be noted, however, that on the question of sectional co-operation the senior students of Pretoria, Heidelberg and Johannesburg recorded a larger percentage of votes against co-operation than their juniors.

In regard to the use of propaganda in schools a larger percentage of senior students at Pretoria and Heidelberg voted in favour than of the juniors. The position was reversed at Johannesburg, where no fourth-year students voted in favour of the use of propaganda, while 7 per cent of the third-year students did so. But bearing in mind the small numbers we are here dealing with, it will not be incorrect to state that the length of training does not appear to make for more liberal views on "racial" co-operation or for an increased dislike of the use by teachers of propaganda in the schools.

It would therefore appear, subject to the limitations of the data which are for the Transvaal only, that among students in Afrikaans medium institutions a prejudice against "racial," or better "sectional," co-operation is accompanied by a desire to use the school for the spreading of propaganda. Among students from the English medium Normal College this does not appear to be the case.

CHAPTER X

THE ROLE OF THE SCHOOL AND THE TEACHER

"To an extent characteristic of no other institution, save that of the State itself, the school has power to modify the social order."

JOHN DEWEY

THE IMPORTANCE OF THE TEACHER. The reason why we discussed the attainments and attitudes of student-teachers in training at such length is because we consider the teacher to be the most important single influence in the school. As the teacher is, so will the school be. The thoughts and opinions of student-teachers in our Normal Colleges to-day will be the thoughts and opinions of our youth twenty to thirty years from now. If we want to start with educational reforms, the Normal College is the chief place to begin with.

By the very nature of our internal social constitution to-day there are minority groups in nearly all South African communities. With the increased mobility of our population due to the war and to increased industrialization, purely homogeneous communities are more and more becoming the exception. And where there are minorities there are bound to be problems which require handling with understanding and tact in the educational field. Given the right type of teacher with an appreciation of the points of view of both sections of our South African community, most of the causes of friction in our schools will be anticipated and forestalled. Where however the teacher himself (particularly the principal) suffers from an inferiority complex due to a one-sided development and training, his school is bound to become a focus of "racial" trouble—if not for himself immediately, insulated as he is in an artificial way, then in any case ultimately for the community at large.

It cannot be denied that in the past there was often discrimination against, and lack of recognition of, minority groups. Our educational history presents many such instances, particularly where the English group was the majority and the Afrikaans group the minority. The trouble generally lay with the staff, in particular with the principal who was unilingual in most cases and who, if not openly unsympathetic, nevertheless made no practical effort to make the minority group feel that it "belonged." Hardly ever, not even in the upper standards, did an English unilingual principal recognize Afrikaans to the extent of making it at least a partial medium in a few subjects in his school. (A change in this attitude has been noticed in a few cases recently.)

Such unenlightened and unsympathetic principals were in any case gradually becoming anachronisms, and the obvious course was to get rid of them in the course of time, and to train men and women who would not only be bilingual, but who would also be imbued with a spirit of co-operation as well as of appreciation of the other section's needs and aspirations.

THE WRONG SOLUTION. Instead of this long-range solution, the position was declared to be impossible, and a course following the line of least resistance was adopted, namely to herd both children and teachers into separate camps wherever possible. Certain Normal Colleges, such as those in the Transvaal, became separate and unilingual institutions. Thus the real difficulty was sidestepped. Teachers found secluded havens where they could be unilingual with impunity and could foster unchecked inbreeding of their own particular type of one-sided citizenship. The narrow, self-complacent products (pupils and teachers) of this inbreeding may be said to be fast developing the attitude of mind typified by the man who prayed:

> "God bless me and my wife,
> Our son John and his wife,
> Us four and no more!"

These colleges are the vested interests which will take a lot of shaking up before any reform can take place.

Salary scales should be improved so as to attract and hold men who are properly equipped to carry the increased responsibilities required. But the ostrich-like lack of courage and vision which caused the present system to develop has caught us up in a vicious circle: on the one hand, inadequate training for our teachers, and on the other, the resultant failure to train our children for complete South African citizenship. It is our children who are paying the penalty of this shortsightedness.

Through deliberate administrative action the bulk of our children, from whom our future teachers have to be drawn, are sent to separate unilingual medium schools. To be trained as a teacher the South African child goes from there to a unilingual medium university and normal college. The chances therefore of his learning to associate with and understand his fellow South Africans of the opposite language group are reduced to a minimum. In many cases the only mental picture which he has of his fellow South Africans is the distorted version presented by a one-sided daily press. He learns to think in terms of labels and clichés instead of in terms of warm and intimate contacts. By this procedure is bred the very type of teacher and principal against whose original one-sidedness the establishment of separate unilingual medium schools was a reaction and formed a supposed remedy. Our educational administration definitely took the wrong turning here. It was a case of putting the clock back with a vengeance. The cumulative effect of this policy of separation, if consistently pursued, will be the existence of two sets of people in South Africa who neither speak the same language nor have common concepts and attitudes regarding human association. By persisting in this direction we are already creating a situation in which the two sections are wearing themselves out in a welter of friction arising out of petty, sectional jealousies, due chiefly to misunderstanding and suspicion. It was the result of this unfortunate condition which the late Professor Drennan foresaw when he wrote: "The South African's Epitaph":

Here lie
Oom Jan and *John Afrikaner Bull*
Two Cousins. Both Fools.
They fought all their lives to find out which was the better man.
They never found out.
This stone was erected with cheerful enthusiasm by the
Bantu Burial Board.

TRAINING IN SOUTH AFRICANISM

The bilingual school presupposes bilingual teachers (see Stage IV, Chapter I). This is the crux of the whole matter. There is, however, ample proof that the bilingual principal in a bilingual school is not a vain and idle dream. There are quite a few such principals, but they are unfortunately getting rarer. Let me quote one example to illustrate my main point. In the Boys' High School at Stellenbosch, as it was conducted under the principalship of Mr. Paul Roos, the dual-medium principle was partially in vogue in the classroom. Outside the classroom the two languages were on a footing of equality. One week all the notices, the announcements at assembly and the prayers were conducted in English. The next week everything was in Afrikaans. To sing the hymns and read the Bible in the two languages in this way not only gave an insight into the traditions and cultural background of the other section, but also enriched the pupil's vocabulary in the second language in a way that the ordinary text-book methods seldom do. On the playground the boys, irrespective of their home language, played in the same teams and heard each other's language in a natural and concrete setting. They got to know each other and to appreciate each other's prowess in work and play. Many lifelong friendships between members of the two sections were built up in that school. When I tested the boys, I noticed no trace of an inferiority feeling among members of the minority group. On the contrary, in the attitude tests this school showed a very high degree of understanding and tolerance between the two sections.[1]

What made all this possible? One of the main factors was undoubtedly the fact that Mr. Roos was the kind of man he was. He was

---

[1] The total results for all bilingual schools taken together showed much the same.

essentially a sportsman. Having been in his younger days captain of the 1906 Springbok rugby team that brought South Africa so prominently into the international limelight on the playing fields of Great Britain, he was used to having under him in the same team both English and Afrikaans-speaking players. They were united by such a fine team-spirit that it did not matter who scored the try or kicked the goal, as long as it was South Africa that won the day. In the eyes of the British, too, they were all South Africans who played for South Africa.

The ideal is clear, inspiring and entirely feasible, provided the will to co-operate exists. Is it reasonable, in the fashion of protagonists of the separatist ideal, to consider such a Springbok team and similar associations constituted of members from both sections as "neither fish, flesh, nor fowl, nor good red herring," or to describe Mr. Roos disparagingly as a "mixed-grill Afrikaner"? The answer is obviously no, since such associations are not only eminently desirable but also essentially practicable.

I have had first-hand experience of this in many ways, for South Africa is full of such instances. To illustrate, let me quote more examples. I travelled with the last Springbok rugby team, which toured Australia and New Zealand under the captaincy of Philip Nel. Though the team was composed of English and Afrikaans-speaking members, both languages were in constant use, with the result that at the end of the tour there was no one who did not speak both fluently. They did not score English tries or Afrikaans tries, but each point scored was for South Africa. And there was no question ever about the essential unity and 100 per cent team-spirit of these men.

SOUTH AFRICANISM IN THE ARMY. The next illustration of active and real co-operation by large numbers of men drawn from both sections is the South African Army. The proportion is about 50/50 Afrikaans and English home language, with a slight preponderance on the Afrikaans side. In the case of our troops up North the proportion of Afrikaans to English-speaking troops has been estimated as high as 60/40.

Thousands of soldiers, especially English-speaking men and women, discovered their "South African" identity for the first time when they joined in the fight for South Africa, and especially when they found themselves separated by vast distances of time and space from their homeland. The urge to assert this South African identity is common to both Afrikaans and English-speaking members of the U.D.F. In living, working, fighting, suffering, dying or triumphing together, they have much to unite and nothing to divide them.

These are not my own opinions but those voiced to me by the soldiers themselves. In my capacity as Director of Military Intelligence, I am responsible for the censorship of soldiers' letters. Through the Army Education Services of which I am in charge I come in daily contact with the views of the troops as individuals and as units. And I have found that this general insistence in their letters and verbal contacts on the common identity conferred upon them by a common background, tradition and homeland, is one of the most significant developments in the recent evolution of South African inter-sectional relationships. It is as if a new synthesis has been achieved. Different cultural origins, different names, separate language media, are acknowledged and accepted, but have no more significance for South African soldiers than the composition of the American people has for a citizen of the United States. The Orange Flash is the badge of their identity.

Contact between the South African forces and the other allied Armies such as the New Zealanders, Australians or men from the British Isles, does not have the effect, as might be expected, of luring away the English-speaking South Africans from the ties which unite them in common association with the Afrikaans-speaking South Africans. Instead of blood and language inspiring him to alignment with fellow Britishers from the Isles and elsewhere, the opposite process rather was observed. In fact the South Africans (English and Afrikaans-speaking) are inclined to stick together in almost a clannish way—which is no more than is to be expected from people who have only just become fully conscious of a distinct and separate nationhood.

Never since the Union has the consciousness of a common heritage dawned so vividly upon such a large and representative number of our South African people as is the case in the South African Army. From thousands of miles away the South African soldier, English and Afrikaans-speaking alike, turns a nostalgic eye homewards—to South Africa. In the midst of strange surroundings, strange customs and usages, strange languages, he turns to familiar things for comfort. He discovers that Afrikaans songs, speech and literature, for instance, interpret better than anything else the sights, sounds and background which for him spell home—South Africa. And we find the English-speaking soldier singing, speaking and reading Afrikaans with natural enthusiasm and confidence. Far from "conceding" their existence, he has simply appropriated these media of expression as part of his South African heritage. In fact, in many cases it was regarded as "good form" to speak Afrikaans. A benevolent conspiracy of circumstances has bestowed on the South African soldier the privilege, ironically denied to the polished, carefully nurtured, and self-appointed apostles of Afrikaans-*kultuur*, of being the first to speak, sing and write in Afrikaans, in parts of the world where people know very little about South Africa and possibly nothing at all about an Afrikaans language.

As was shown in the previous chapters, the Afrikaans-speaking South African is more bilingual than the English-speaking South African in the sense that he has developed his second language further. This deficiency has been felt acutely by many South African soldiers, who have ascribed it to lack of opportunity of hearing Afrikaans. The Army now, like a huge melting-pot, has thrown English and Afrikaans-speaking men and women together in a common association they have never known before, and out of this has come a gain in bilingualism which is chiefly a gain in Afrikaans. And if there is one thing the men in the Army are unanimous about, it is giving their children the opportunities of becoming bilingual which they missed in their youth.

WE LEARN TO CO-OPERATE BY CO-OPERATING. But what is more, the men have been engaged on a job together. Bravery, reliability and skill were appreciated, irrespective of a man's home language, which soon became an irrelevant consideration when there was a job to be done. The same is true with children. The best solution therefore seems to be in the direction of multiplying the situations under which children actually live together and thereby learn to co-operate as South Africans in the first instance. To keep them systematically apart as if they were representatives of two entirely different and strange nations is to ignore the basic facts of South African life and to store up great potential trouble for future generations. Our practical daily work in commerce, industry, farming and the professions, as well as our geographic interspersion, demands the closest association of the two sections, and the school should recognize that fact and prepare men and women for such a reality.

Moreover, as our figures show, it is no longer correct to speak of the two sections as if they were entirely separate. An ever-increasing common element is growing up which is as much a reality and a factor to be reckoned with in our national life as the two extreme ends of the home language spectrum (see the Graph on p. 48). In fact, if the school does its job properly these two extremities will gradually dwindle and become the exception, as the middle zones consisting of the bilingual home language groups expand and become the regular and accepted thing in South African life.

SOUTH AFRICANIZATION. Just as Americanization has been set up as one of the main objectives of the American school, so South Africanization should become the objective for the South African school. Just as the American Government insists on the learning of English by every school child, and the use of that language as the main instrument in achieving Americanization, so the South African Government should insist on the learning of *both* languages, and on their use as media in the school. Some people may doubt on psychological grounds whether two common languages in a bilingual country can weld a people into one nation as effectively as one single language. "Die taal is gansch het volk," as a great Flemish leader once said. One cannot be dogmatic about this question, but we have at any rate the example of a trilingual country like Switzerland. Nobody who has been to that country and has studied its history would dare to stamp the Swiss as lacking in patriotism and solidarity on the one hand or in achievement in the fields of science, culture and literature on the other.

To maintain that no nation can be either united or great unless its culture is limited to only *one* language is to be blind to the facts of history. Even in ancient times, as Prof. Haarhoff has so convincingly shown in his book, *The Stranger at the Gate*, the Roman Empire reached the zenith of its achievements as a result of its life and thought being enriched by the culture of two languages, Greek as well as Latin.

What makes a nation, as Renan has said, is the knowledge of having done great things together in the past, and the *will* to do things together in the future. We do not make enough in our history teaching of the great things which South Africans have done together, e.g. the Act of Union, and in a smaller way, our Agricultural Unions, "Child Welfare" and other organizations to promote social welfare. We are too apt to dwell on the things on which we were divided and over which we fought each other. Surely that is the crux of the whole question. It is the *will* to do things together. If that will is lacking then we can only foresee uncoordinated action, division and disintegration. And the only way to strengthen that will is to give to every child the opportunity to share in the common experience of the whole nation and not to penalize him by isolating him in a corner or in a section. This is where the bilingual school comes in. While it may not be practicable to make it universal right away, it is the direction in which we should steer.

MERE BILINGUALISM IS NOT ENOUGH. Mere proficiency in the second language is no guarantee in itself that a child will, *ipso facto*, have a feeling of unity or co-operate amicably with his fellow South Africans. Our bilingual survey gave us evidence that this does not necessarily follow, for there are cases in unilingual Afrikaans medium city schools where a fairly high proficiency in English was found concomitant with very extreme feelings of antipathy against the English-speaking section. This proficiency is not so much due to the efforts of the school in question as to the effect of the city environment which is predominantly English. Everything depends on the circumstances under which the language is learnt. As Prof. Pierre Bovet of Geneva pointed out at the South African Conference of the New Education Fellowship in 1934, when speaking on Bilingualism in the different parts of the world: "Everything depends on the context in which the second language is presented to the child and assimilated by him. . . . School bilingualism may take very different shades according as the language used in school is a language eagerly sought after, or the language of a nation feared, hated or despised." The emotional atmosphere is of great importance. It must be favourable if the language is to serve as a means of social integration. The more natural the process, i.e. the more it approaches that by which a child picks up a language from a playmate or from his environment, the less will be the emotional conflict and the more effective the learning process.

Here the teacher's method and attitude are also of paramount importance. A certain teacher in an Afrikaans medium class introducing the English lesson sighed and said: "Kom kinders, laat ons nou weer vir'n uur gaan worstel met die vyand se taal." (Come children, let us now wrestle again for an hour with the enemy's language.) In an English medium school, on the other hand, I personally heard the master refer to Afrikaans as "kitchen Dutch," and subsequently as a "bastard language."

Needless to say in both these schools the achievement in the second language was poor. But even though the teacher were to wrestle ever so effectively with the second language so that the children achieved high marks in the public examinations, bilingualism with such a background would not by itself automatically achieve social integration but would probably bring about the exact opposite.

CHAPTER XI

SOME EDUCATIONAL PRINCIPLES

IN conclusion we shall summarize the main educational principles underlying the point of view expressed in the foregoing chapters. Some of these principles are of a psychological nature and are concerned chiefly with the role of language in the learning process; others are of a sociological nature and deal more particularly with the functions of language and of the school as institutions for bringing about social integration.

It is taken for granted that the school must assist the child in interpreting his environment and in organizing his experiences in such a way that he develops what is known as character or personality. In order to perform this function adequately the school must do two things: (i) utilize the child's environment in the learning process to the fullest extent (this is the justification for home language medium); (ii) compensate the child for the deficiencies of his environment. It is only when environment and school supplement each other that the school can serve as a means of social integration as well as of individual development.

1. THE UTILIZATION OF ENVIRONMENT

One of the fundamental principles of teaching is the effective use by the school of the child's environment in imparting knowledge. In educational method one goes from the relatively known to the relatively unknown. Indeed, this is the educational justification for teaching the young child through the language he understands best. The early education of many Afrikaans-speaking adults in the early days was a laborious affair, for it involved the use of two relatively strange languages, English and Dutch, as media of instruction—both opaque media compared with the transparent, flexible Afrikaans which we spoke at home but which had not yet been recognized as a medium or as a language in our schools. It was a case of learning the unknown through the unknown right from the start—obviously an educationally unsound and wasteful process. To-day, fortunately, the situation is vastly changed and this sort of thing is hardly found any more.

To-day also the environment of the South African child outside the school has become more bilingual. Not only in school does every South African child learn both languages as subjects, but in the case of fully 50 per cent they hear and use both languages outside school, i.e. at home and in the street. That fact should be fully utilized by the school and on that experience of the child his education should be built. This makes for economy in the learning process and is probably the reason why bilingual children do better in the bilingual school than in the unilingual school. Their whole experience is utilized in the learning process and not merely part of it.

Where a community consists of Afrikaans-speaking as well as English-speaking children who live within the vicinity of a particular school, there is according to this principle no good reason why the potential fund of linguistic experience of that community should not be capitalized and made available in that school by bringing them together in one institution. On the playground and in the general assembly the young child from a unilingual home can then at least hear the second language *spoken* by other children. This, as every language teacher knows, greatly enhances the work in the second language lessons.

In communities where the second language is not used at all and where the school, from the nature of the circumstances, has to be unilingual (at least in the elementary stages), the school has to supply the second language experience all on its own—a very difficult task indeed—requiring bilingual teachers of a high grade. This brings us to the second function of the school.

2. THE ENRICHMENT OF ENVIRONMENT

Not only should the school utilize and interpret to the child his environment but it should also compensate him for the deficiencies of the immediate environment. Then and then only can it function as a truly educational and national institution.

Environments are naturally limitative and deterministic in their effect on the individual. They are all the more so in proportion as they are inescapable. In a young country like South Africa young men and women can be expected to function in any part of it. For its satisfactory development mobility of its citizens is essential. They should not be tied down by lack of preparation or opportunity; otherwise social stagnation and economic deterioration will result. This was, as I showed in my *Education and the Poor White*, one of the chief causes of Poor Whitism in South Africa. Our rural people suffer from *soul erosion* as well as from soil erosion.

The school is the only institution which if properly run can offer us a long-range but sure solution. According to this principle it should give the child, no matter where he lives, as full a chance as possible of participating in the life of the people as a whole. If the school does anything less, it sends the child out with a feeling of inferiority which is detrimental to his character and personality in the long run. It is therefore an essential function of the school to make up for the deficiencies in the child's spiritual and mental background. That is what we establish schools for. Otherwise we could have left every child merely to the mercies of home and street environment to pick up whatever learning he might. But we spend annually over £10,000,000 out of State funds on the education of our white children in South Africa, because we believe in this compensatory function of the school in building South African citizens.

It must be remembered further that these schools are run for the children and not for the convenience of teachers. Now if it is proved, and we think it has been conclusively demonstrated, that we can only meet the real needs of our children by making the bilingual school the rule and the unilingual school the exception (instead of the other way about as it is becoming to-day), the parents of this country should have the courage of their convictions and demand bilingual schools. Even if the bilingual school should present organizational and time-table difficulties and exact more thought and planning from the teachers and the education departments, we should still demand it. In education it is after all the interests of the children and not administrative convenience which should be our first consideration.

THE HANDICAPS DUE TO ENVIRONMENT OUTSIDE HOME AND SCHOOL. The need of the school in South Africa as a compensating agency in deficient environments is nowhere more evident than in the field of the two official languages. To illustrate this, I present the following table and graph showing the wide discrepancies between the scores in the second language by children in the same standards due to different environments: (a) City, (b) Town, (c) Rural. These figures show clearly the potency of the child's environment outside the schoolroom and even outside the home in determining the child's achievement in the second language. We are dealing here only with Afrikaans home language pupils.

SCORES IN ENGLISH BY AFRIKAANS HOME LANGUAGE PUPILS IN
AFRIKAANS MEDIUM SCHOOLS

Standard			City	Town	Rural
IV	..	..	..	298	233	157
V	..	..	..	347	315	221
VI	..	..	..	387	345	245
VII	..	..	..	440	420	316
VIII	..	..	..	505	460	368
Average			395	355	261

It will be remembered from a previous chapter that 66 points represents on an average roughly one school standard in language progress. From the above table it will be seen that on an average the Afrikaans medium children in the *town* schools are 60 points (i.e nearly a year) behind the Afrikaans medium children in the *city* schools, while rural children are 94 points (i.e. nearly a year and a half) behind the town children in their second language, English. Taking the individual standards and looking at Graph X it will be seen, for example, that the Standard VIII rural child's English is considerably below that of the Standard VI city child : i.e. he is more than two whole standards behind his Afrikaans cousin in the city.

GRAPH X

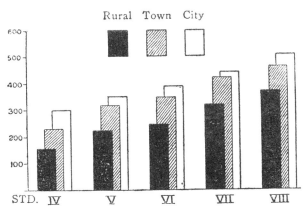

Graph showing the widely different attainments in English by Afrikaans children in the same standards according to the situation of their schools (*a*) in a rural area, (*b*) in a town, or (*c*) in a city. This illustrates the potency of the linguistic environment outside the home. For these are all Afrikaans home language children. The wide differences must therefore be due largely to the widely divergent opportunities for hearing the second language in these different environments. (Note : 66 points on the scale represents one whole school year's progress.) It is for this reason that we have laid such great stress on the function of the school as a means of compensating the child for the deficiencies of his environment.

The Standard IV child in the city is nearly as good in English as the Standard VII rural child, i.e. the latter is nearly three standards behind the urban child in the same standard. It is probably true that the quality of English teaching in rural schools is inferior on the average to that in the city and town schools, where specialist teachers are generally employed for these subjects. But that is not the only factor operative here.[1]

[1] The superiority of teachers' qualifications here is, however, only relative and not very large. Actually the quality of English teaching in Afrikaans medium schools is poorer than that of Afrikaans in English medium schools, especially in the rural schools.

The quality of second language teaching was objectively measured on a 10-point scale based on the following points. The weights given to each are shown in brackets.

      (*a*) Academic qualifications of language teacher   (1)
      (*b*) Professional qualifications of language teacher   (2)
      (*c*) Language qualifications of language teacher   (3)
      (*d*) Home language qualifications of language teacher (2)
      (*e*) Principals' ratings of language teachers   (2)

The question arises: Is it fair that the rural child should be so severely penalized in learning his second language simply because he does not live in a town or a city while he goes to school? He surely has as much right to become a bilingual citizen and to compete as regards bilinguality on an equal footing with his Afrikaans cousin in the city or town when it comes to looking for a job later on in life. It is not advisable for all rural boys and girls to stay on the farms. Poor Whitism has largely been caused by the redundant rural population staying on the land. And our survey of the records of the Juvenile Affairs Boards show how good, capable boys and girls from the platteland are handicapped by lack of English when looking for work in the city.

3. THE SCHOOL A REFLECTION OF THE LIFE OF THE COMMUNITY AS A WHOLE

The public school to be effective in a democratic country like South Africa should reflect the structure of the community it serves. It should reflect the structure of the community as a whole and not merely that of a section. If a sectional or parochial point of view is to be advanced through means of the school, that section is free to establish its own schools, provided it is prepared to pay for those schools itself. It should not, however, use the State's schools to further its own parochial ends. That is why certain religious denominations, like the Roman Catholic Church, in South Africa and in other countries like the U.S.A., with big public school systems, establish their own schools as parochial or private institutions for which they pay out of Church funds.

In South Africa, however, we as a people do not favour the private or parochial school. We send over 95 per cent of the children of the country to public schools which are supported out of State funds. Recently there has been a strong movement on foot by the Dutch Reformed Church to repudiate the bilingual school and to appropriate the unilingual Afrikaans medium school as its own particular charge, chiefly on religious grounds. There are clear signs that it wishes to dominate all Afrikaans medium institutions as if they were its own sectarian institutions. The difference however is that instead of paying for such schools itself, the Dutch Reformed Church now wishes to utilize State schools for its own ends, presumably thereby hoping to retain its denominational hold on the people.

But it has not been proved that the bilingual school is in any way less religious (or even less Christian) than the unilingual school according to the principles of religious teaching embodied in the educational ordinances. The assumptions underlying this attitude are also not only inconsistent with, but represent a complete departure from, the centuries-old attitude of the Dutch Reformed Church towards the State school in South Africa.

For the disinterestedness of the Dutch Reformed Church from a denominational point of view in furthering the State school has been often remarked upon by superintendents and administrators of education. I have myself recounted[1] the many outstanding services which the Dutch Reformed Church rendered to State education and am therefore in a better position than most people to state that the recent trend in the Church's attitude as manifested by the agitation of its leaders is something quite foreign to the fine tradition of disinterested service to the community as a whole rendered by so many of its ministers.

In any case, in this controversy concerning the respective merits of the bilingual and the unilingual school, denominationalism is something wholly irrelevant and in fairness to both the Church and the school should not be dragged in. The fact of the matter is that South Africa is a bilingual country, and its children, no matter what their home language may be to start with, are destined to associate with each other in nearly every kind of political, social and economic activity when they grow up. To prepare children for this life the State school in South Africa should not only recognize this fact but should be the South African community in miniature, as John Dewey would put it. Only in this way can it be an institution designed to educate the complete South African citizen.

4. LEARN BY DOING

The last fundamental principle is that children learn by doing. (1) They learn a language best by using it, especially when they feel the need for using it in concrete life-situations. (2) They learn to co-operate by actually co-operating and not by talking in the abstract about co-operation and national unity while being herded into separate kraals and not being given a chance to live out that ideal in practical life. As regards his cultural life, man is almost totally a creature of habit and it is on that level that we have to approach the problem in practice. Let us first look at language. For our present purpose we may distinguish three main functions of language (obviously they are interrelated): (*a*) As a medium through which learning and instruction takes place. (*b*) As a means of artistic expression in the field of literature. (*c*) As a means of social intercourse and integration.

(*a*) LANGUAGE AS A MEDIUM FOR LEARNING. Language is the chief vehicle by which the accumulated experience of the older generation is transmitted to the younger. It is essentially a set of symbols, of gestures, sounds and letters, which in course of time acquire meaning for the growing child. Of course a good deal of a child's learning or experience takes place initially through direct sensory contact and muscular sensations without the intermediary of the symbols which we call words or

---

[1] See *Education in South Africa, 1652–1922*, pp. 109 ff. My series of articles: "Die Bydrae van die N. G. Kerk tot die Onderwys in South Africa," published in *Die Kerkbode*, deel xx, Okt. en Nov. 1927.

H

language. Every child is born into an environment which is full of such symbols. Sometimes these symbols belong to one system, as in a unilingual environment. Sometimes they belong to two or more systems—these being usually differentiated by being associated respectively with different sets of persons or certain specific situations. This is the case in a bilingual or a multilingual environment. This is how the young child distinguishes one language from another in such an environment. And experiments have shown that young children, growing up in bilingual environments, do not confuse the two languages if these are used in two distinct "universes of discourse," e.g. the father consistently speaking one language to the child and the mother the other language, as in the famous case described by Ronjat;[1] or the child hearing one language from his parents, another from the servants and still another from his playmates—as frequently happens in the Transvaal and Natal where the Bantu languages are often used with Native servants. If these "universes of discourse" are kept consistently distinct, children hardly ever mix their languages. It is when they hear adults mixing languages that they mix them too and that a certain confusion results.

Bilingualism and Mental Development. Now one sometimes hears doubts expressed about the mental development of children growing up bilingually. Some even go so far as to say that because a bilingual child has to learn two names for a certain thing instead of one, his mental growth is halved. This claim has no foundation in fact. To claim further, as Jespersen[2] does, that "the brain effort required to master two languages instead of one certainly diminishes the child's power of learning other things" is, as Arsenian[3] rightly points out, going beyond the known facts. Such a claim is based on what I would call the "box-theory" of the human mind. This theory is held by those who picture the human mind as a box which can hold just so much and no more, so that if certain new facts or a new subject are put in, the others get pushed out. These people contend, for example, that the use of the second language (in the way suggested in Chapter II) as a language or as a medium takes up the space in the child's brain which is required either for the first language or for the subject matter, e.g. geography or history.

But the human spirit is no such mechanical contraption. It is an organic growth with all the flexibility characteristic of an organism. We know actually too little about human capacity to put such arbitrary limits to man's powers of assimilation. The main point is: there must be the will or the urge to learn. Besides, as Arsenian points out, there is no assurance that the monoglot child, who has more free time at his disposal than the bilingual child according to Jespersen's argument,

---

[1] *Le Développement du Langage observé chez un Enfant Bilingue.* (Paris, 1913.)
[2] O. Jespersen, *Language, its Nature, Development and Origin* (New York, 1922), p. 148.
[3] Arsenian, *Bilingualism and Mental Development,* p. 133.

will use that time for useful purposes. Ordinarily men learn when they have to.

The point we wish to stress here is that, in proportion as a child in a bilingual environment comes into contact with the two sets of symbols as part of his daily experience, in that same proportion are they to him media through which his learning processes take place. The fact that words for the same thing in two different languages never mean exactly the same but often have slightly different shades or nuances, would seem to imply that the experience of the bilingual child, being drawn from the two sets of symbols contained in a bilingual environment, would be enriched in meaning by the dual contact.

In any case, if one surveys the best experimental evidence on the question, e.g. the work by Ronjat,[1] Pavlovitch,[2] McCarthy,[3] Schiller[4] and Arsenian, one finds no scientific proof of the assumed mental inferiority of bilingual children. Arsenian formulates his conclusion thus: "The acquisition of two language systems by the bilingualist in place of one system, as is the case with the monoglot, does not seem from the data of the present study to have a detrimental influence on mental ability and development."[5]

(b) LANGUAGE AS LITERATURE. Language is also a means of artistic expression, i.e. through poetry and prose. It is the vehicle which carries the nation's literature. Only the chosen few in every people are given the ability to use language with such excellence in embodying worthwhile thoughts that their literary products live as literature in the minds and hearts of the people. The question to what extent this is possible of attainment by people with a bilingual background has already been touched upon in Chapter I and need not detain us here.

We are, however, concerned primarily with the bulk of the population; and the main point here is that, whether a child is bilingual or not, it is the function of the South African school to see to it that he is properly disciplined throughout his school career in expressing himself clearly, concisely and happily in whichever of the two languages he uses. This discipline comes by actual use of the language. The interesting point which emerges from our investigation as well as from the experience of many good writers is that, if the discipline in the one language is sound, it need not be impaired by the use of the other in other "universes of discourse" (even in the initial stages). On the contrary a certain language sense or sensitivity for the use of words seems to be developed.

(c) LANGUAGE AS A MEANS OF SOCIAL INTEGRATION. Just as one set of

---

[1] Ronjat, *Le Développement du Langage observé chez un Enfant Bilingue.*
[2] Pavlovitch, *La Langue Enfantine* (Paris, 1920).
[3] McCarthy, *The Language Development of the Pre-School Child* (Minneapolis, 1930).
[4] Schiller, "Verbal, Numerical and Spatial Abilities of Young Children," *Archives of Psychology* (New York, 1934).
[5] Arsenian, *Bilingualism and Mental Development*, p. 143.

symbols in a unilingual country serves as a means of binding a people together, so it should not be impossible for two sets of symbols when they have become the common possession of all the people in that group to function similarly as an instrument for social integration.

As Carlton Hayes put it (*Essays on Nationalism* (New York, 1926), p. 16) "Uniformity of language tends to promote like-mindedness, to provide an inclusive set of ideas as well as of words, and like-minded persons tend to develop group-consciousness, to experience a sense of common interest, to constitute a tribe or nationality. Members of such a group naturally regard persons who speak a strange and alien language as 'unlike' or different from themselves and hence as inferior and not entitled to belong to themselves."

THE ONLY PRACTICAL WAY

In order to be effective as a means of social integration the two official languages in South Africa must be acquired through mutual association of the individuals concerned and not merely by learning either of them *in vacuo* from a book. Our investigations show that the best results are gained by using them in concrete situations. Language is essentially an instrument which improves by use in as widely divergent situations as possible. To confine the learning of the second language therefore to one period a day, when it is learnt as a subject and is usually treated in a formal and unreal fashion, is not only educationally wasteful but also places a handicap on children socially and politically which prevents them from participating with complete freedom as citizens in South African life.

We have already stressed the point that a mere knowledge of the second language does not automatically bring with it the desire to co-operate with the other section. This was shown in our results where a relatively high attainment in English by children of the unilingual Afrikaans medium school in the cities was accompanied by a high degree of antagonism towards the English section. On the other hand, a poor average score in Afrikaans in unilingual medium English schools in the city was accompanied by a very low degree of discrimination against the Afrikaans section. If bilingualism therefore is to serve as a means of social integration, something more than the mere study of the second language as a subject is needed. Personal contact by learning, playing and living together is what is required. Then, and then only, will the second language become a real thing for the child and be able to serve as an adequate means of social integration. And where the geographic distribution of our people requires it, as in rural areas which are predominantly Afrikaans-speaking and urban areas which are predominantly English-speaking, facilities should be multiplied by which there can be inter-school exchange of pupils (particularly as boarders), and where pupils can visit each other's homes in urban and rural areas. A special organization for handling this should be set up in each education department.

There are many people who think that the cultivation of bilingualism should be postponed until the High School stage, which is the usual place for the introduction of modern languages. That may be feasible where the second language is a foreign language, e.g. French or German or Italian, but it is absurd to do that with a language of the country itself. In the first place, the earlier a child starts the more easily he picks up a language; and in the second place, 40 per cent of all our children who leave school do not study further than Standard VI and 60 per cent do not go beyond Standard VII. Only about 10 per cent ever pass matriculation, and less than half of these go to University.

The large majority of our children, therefore, never reach the High School proper. We stress these figures because we find that few people realize that for the majority of our future citizens the primary school offers the only chance of attaining a knowledge of the second language, in so far as the school can give it. In many areas it is only the school that can give it. This applies to English as well as Afrikaans. It is for this reason that we so strongly stress the compensatory function of the school.

We still need a good deal of scientific experimentation in varying environments to find out the best method by which the second language should be introduced, not only as a subject but when used as a partial medium, so as to interfere as little as possible with the child's learning process in the content subjects even in the initial stages. Luckily, however, the results so far obtained show clearly that it need no longer be a choice between two evils: loss of a second language on the one hand or loss of content on the other.

The evidence from other countries, as well as our own observations, point clearly to one crucial factor, namely the importance of the method by which these measures are put into effect and of the mental attitude engendered in the child in the process. If the attitude is a natural and unprejudiced one, such as one finds when children, engrossed in the process of playing together, pick up languages from each other, the introduction of the second language (as a language or as a medium— for there is at this stage really not much difference) has no deleterious effects either on the child's mental or moral development. If, however, this learning of the second language is associated with compulsion and emotional conflict, it may have adverse effects on the development of the child's personality. The degree of this harm depends entirely on the extent to which the child finds himself involved in such conflict, whether it is in the home between parents, or in the school with the teacher, or outside the school between sections of the community which impinge upon his experience.

A great responsibility therefore rests upon the child's parents in the first instance, and upon the child's teachers, not to project their conflicts and prejudices (acquired under conditions which have long since changed) upon the young children entrusted to their care. The next generation must be given a fair chance to move freely upward on the difficult path towards greater national unity—unhampered by the blocks and shackles of our prejudices and animosities acquired in a troubled past. *Ut per juvenes ascendat mundus*—"Let the world keep moving upward through its youth."

CHAPTER XII

SUMMARY OF THE MAIN CONCLUSIONS

SOUTH AFRICA IS A BILINGUAL COUNTRY

1. The bilingual situation in South Africa is unique and not comparable with that in other bilingual countries. Therefore arguments based on the practice in other countries are very often not valid. According to the Union Census figures about 66 per cent of our white population to-day speak both official languages as compared with only 13 per cent in Canada, for example. Moreover, in South Africa the two language groups are much more geographically interspersed than in other countries and the number of children coming to school with a bilingual background is considerable and is steadily increasing. (See p. 17.)

2. The Union Census figures for 1936 showed that (a) 16 per cent spoke Afrikaans only; (b) 64 per cent spoke both English and Afrikaans; (c) 19 per cent spoke English only. (See p. 17.)

3. The Orange Free State, with 69 per cent speaking both languages, is the most bilingual of the four provinces, and Natal with 44 per cent the least. The most bilingual towns in South Africa are Bloemfontein with 75 per cent and Pretoria with 73 per cent. The most unilingual towns are Durban with 33 per cent, Pietermaritzburg with 42 per cent and East London with 51 per cent. Cape Town with 63 per cent and the Rand with 60 per cent lie more or less in between.

4. A larger percentage speaking both official languages is found in the communities that are predominantly Afrikaans than in the predominantly English communities. (See p. 49.)

5. Our tests also show that in every school standard the bilingual quotients of Afrikaans pupils are consistently higher than those of English pupils. (See p. 66.)

6. Though the percentage of those able to speak both languages has increased from 40 per cent to 66 per cent during the last 25 years, the *rate* of increase in the percentage of bilingual South Africans is falling. (See p. 17.) Women are less bilingual than men.

SCHOOL ORGANIZATION IN RELATION TO LANGUAGE IN SOUTH AFRICA

7. (a) As *subjects* both languages are taught to all children in South African schools.

(b) As *medium* of instruction only the home language, that is the language the child understands best, is used in the lower standards. The second language may however be introduced as an additional medium beyond the early stages. In Natal the 1942 Ordinance requires this to be done from Standard II. In the Transvaal it may be done after Standard IV and in the Orange Free State and the Cape after Standard VI. In actual practice this is very seldom done.

(c) In order to give effect to the above regulations, two types of school organization have been evolved:

(1) *The Unilingual Medium School*, where the Afrikaans and English-speaking children are segregated into separate schools and where only one language is used as a medium throughout, except when teaching the second language as a subject.

(2) *The Bilingual Medium School*, where English and Afrikaans-speaking children go to the same school, and provision regarding the medium of instruction is made in three different ways:

(i) The parallel-class system, consisting of English medium classes and Afrikaans medium classes in the same school.

(ii) The dual-medium system by which both media are used alternately in teaching one subject or by teaching some subjects through the one medium and other subjects through the other medium to English and Afrikaans pupils sitting together in the same class.

(iii) A combination of the parallel and dual-medium systems, the former being more common in the lower classes and the latter more common in the upper classes. (See Chapter II.)

THE HOME LANGUAGE MEDIUM PRINCIPLE

8. The home (or family) language medium principle is more strongly entrenched in the educational enactments in South Africa than in any other bilingual country. In Canada (Quebec particularly) the medium is determined according to the child's *religious affiliation* and in Switzerland according to the language of the *town* in which the child lives, irrespective of the language spoken in the home. (See p. 32.)

9. As an educational principle the use of the child's home language as a medium of instruction, especially in the early stages, is sound. Education to be effective must utilize the child's own environment and experience as a foundation on which to build. (See p. 102.)

10. The home language of South African pupils is as follows: (a) 25 per cent Afrikaans only; (b) 43 per cent English and Afrikaans in varying degrees; (c) 32 per cent English only.

11. South African conditions are so complex and the language back-

ground of South African children so much a matter of degree that the blind application of abstract principles based on all-or-none assumptions as regards medium will simply not work out in practice. (See p. 46.)

12. Thus if the home language medium principle were consistently applied in the case of the 43 per cent, instruction should be given through both media in varying degrees. Otherwise the principle of home language or mother-tongue medium would be violated and only a limited portion of these bilingual children's home environment would be utilized as a means of educating them.

MEDIUM OF INSTRUCTION IN RELATION TO HOME LANGUAGE

13. Actually the position works out as follows:

(a) 85·5 per cent of the children with completely unilingual Afrikaans environment receive their instruction through Afrikaans, 5·3 per cent through English and 9·3 per cent through both.

(b) 97·6 per cent of children with completely unilingual English environment receive their instruction through English, 0·3 per cent through Afrikaans and 2·1 per cent through both.

(c) Of the children who hear English and Afrikaans almost equally often in their homes, 45 per cent receive their instruc-through Afrikaans, 50 per cent through English and 5 per cent through both. (See p. 53.)

14. It would seem that the bilingual school with dual-medium instruction would, in the case of the middle group with bilingual home environment, give expression more adequately to the principle of home language medium than the separate schools with single medium throughout into which most of these children are now segregated. There are other considerations, too, which will be mentioned later. The main point here is that for a very considerable number of schoolchildren in South Africa the home language consists of both English and Afrikaans in varying proportions.

It is not, therefore, in keeping with the facts to imply, as is so often done, that when the second language is used as a medium in South Africa the children are being taught through a foreign medium. Afrikaans is not foreign to South African children, neither is English. The situation is by no means parallel to that of the use of French in schools in England for example. (See p. 54.)

THE EFFECT OF THE WRONG MEDIUM ON THE PROGRESS OF PUPILS

15. In the extreme case of the 5 per cent of South African children

with completely unilingual home environment (e.g. Afrikaans) being taught from the beginning solely through the second language as a medium, it is found that these children suffer an initial but not very serious handicap in their content subjects. As they progress to higher standards the medium seems to become of decreasing significance and has no observable adverse effect on their school progress in Standard VI and beyond. In subjects like arithmetic, where language does not play such a big role, the handicap is smaller than in subjects like geography and history, where language plays a greater role in the imparting of knowledge. Incidentally, it may be mentioned that those Afrikaans-speaking children who received their instruction in geography through English medium progressively outstripped those in Afrikaans medium from Standard VII upwards. (See pp. 57, 58.)

16. Whatever handicap there is in the "content" subjects is found to be almost precisely in proportion to the relative strangeness of the language used as medium and is practically non-existent where the child's knowledge of the second language approximates that of his first language. (See p. 57.)

17. As regards languages, it was found in the case of exclusively Afrikaans home language pupils, for example, that owing to the fact that their instruction in Afrikaans was confined to the one period a day when they learnt it as a subject (together with English-speaking children), they were about one-third of a year behind the children who went to Afrikaans medium schools. On the other hand, as a result of using English (i.e. their second language) as a medium they were two years ahead in English. (See p. 56.)

18. The number of children with unilingual home background who thus receive all their instruction through the "wrong" medium is only about 5 per cent of the whole school population. This is therefore the extreme and somewhat exceptional position and must not be confused with the practice which obtains in the bilingual school, where the pupil is taught chiefly through his first language, and only partially through his second language. (See p. 60.)

BILINGUAL AND UNILINGUAL SCHOOLS COMPARED AS REGARDS SCHOLASTIC ACHIEVEMENT

19. Let us now compare children's achievements in unilingual and bilingual schools respectively. In the latter type of school the child, even though he obtains a large part of his instruction through his mother tongue, at least hears the second language in the playground, and when he gets beyond the elementary classes is taught through the second language as a partial though subsidiary medium. In comparing these two groups of children intelligence and home language have been kept constant.

20. As regards language attainment, the superiority in their second

languages both on the part of English and Afrikaans-speaking pupils is considerable where they attend the bilingual school—the English-speaking pupils (being the less bilingual to start with) thereby gaining more in Afrikaans than the Afrikaans-speaking pupils in English. In fact, the gain is more than four times as big. (See p. 63.)

21. In their first language, or mother tongue (whether English or Afrikaans) there is no loss whatsoever on the part of those attending the bilingual school. (See pp. 63, 69.)

22. Our results show that in the South African situation the highest degree of bilingualism (obtained by adding their Afrikaans and English scores together) is attained by bilingual children attending bilingual schools. Next come the bilinguals and Afrikaans home language children attending English medium schools; next bilinguals in Afrikaans medium schools. The lowest on the list are the unilingual home language pupils attending unilingual medium schools where the medium is the same as the home language—English and Afrikaans single medium schools being about equally poor. (See Graph VI, p. 69.)

23. As regards attainment in "content" subjects, it has often been maintained that, while the partial use of the second language as a medium may help the second language, the child loses in "content." This contention has been definitely disproved in the case of the bilingual school where the results in the ordinary subjects are consistently better than those attained by pupils in unilingual schools—intelligence and home language being kept constant in the two types compared. (See p. 73.)

24. There is a theory that while the clever child may survive the use of the second language as a medium, the duller child suffers badly. We therefore made the comparison at different intelligence levels, and found that not only the bright children but also the children below normal intelligence do better school work all round in the bilingual school than in the unilingual school. What is most significant is that the greatest gain for the bilingual school was registered in the second language by the lower intelligence groups. Not only do they more than hold their own in their first language but in their second language their gain was nearly twice as big as that registered by the higher intelligence groups. (See p. 64.)

25. It would seem that the linguistic experience gained by contact with the second language in the playground and in other concrete ways in the bilingual school is vital in the case of the dull child and should be capitalized as a means of learning the second language. Our statistics show that children in the bilingual school actually speak the second language in the playground three times as often as children in the unilingual school. (See p. 65.)

To sum up: Contrary to general expectation, children with low intelligence have a relatively better chance of becoming bilingual citizens (without loss in their mother tongue or in their content subjects) by attending the bilingual school than by attending the unilingual school. (See p. 64.)

26. The English-speaking child, while not losing at all in English, gains four times as much in Afrikaans as the Afrikaans-speaking child in English by attending the bilingual school. This means that by the more general adoption of the dual-medium principle in English schools the relative backwardness which the English-speaking section have thus far had in respect of bilingualism will be wiped out. This will bring with it also a great extension in the speaking, reading and writing of Afrikaans in many spheres of South African life. (See p. 72.)

BACKWARDNESS IN THE SECOND LANGUAGE

27. At present Afrikaans children in unilingual Afrikaans medium schools are about two and a half years behind in English compared standard for standard with English children in English medium schools. Similarly English children in English medium schools are about three years behind in Afrikaans, when compared standard for standard with Afrikaans medium schools. This disparity is considerably lessened where these children from unilingual homes attend bilingual schools.

BILINGUAL CHILDREN SUPERIOR ALL ROUND

28. Throughout these comparisons between two types of school, the bilingual and the unilingual school, one has to keep the home environment factor constant lest one ascribe to the school certain language results which are really due to the influence of environment outside the school. This is important for another reason: it was found that children from more or less bilingual homes are on an average more intelligent than children from purely unilingual homes, whether English or Afrikaans.

29. Bilingual children also reach a higher all-round level of scholastic achievement than unilingual children, whether English or Afrikaans. (See p. 67.)

30. Bilingual children in English medium are about three-fourths of a year ahead in mental growth of bilingual children in Afrikaans medium. This superiority was registered not only in the ordinary intelligence tests, but also in the non-linguistic intelligence test (Beta). This is probably due to selective factors of a social nature which operate in South African society. (See p. 67.)

CHILDREN'S ATTITUDE ON "RACIAL DISCRIMINATION"

31. It has been alleged by those who oppose the bilingual school that by putting pupils of the two sections together in one school the antipathies and prejudices which they might bring in from the home are accentuated, whereas if they go to separate schools friction is avoided

and they learn to respect each other. Our results show the very opposite. What is more, in the bilingual school the prejudices brought from the home which are fairly much in evidence in the early standards steadily diminish as one goes up in the school, so that by the time they reach Standard X the pupils seem to regard themselves more or less as one group bound together by common experiences and common loyalties centering round the school. Sectional feelings which were strong at the start, due to differences in home language origin, seem to recede into the background.[1] Though there are exceptions, this is the general trend which manifests itself in the large majority of cases. (See Graph IX on p. 85.)

32. In this respect no significant differences could be found between the results of the two forms of bilingual school, viz.: the parallel-class form and the dual-medium form. (See p. 78.)

33. Adverse sectional discrimination is from three to four times as great in unilingual schools of all types as in bilingual schools. (See p. 84.)

34. Of the unilingual schools it is greater in the Afrikaans medium than in the English medium schools. While adverse sectional discrimination generally diminishes as children go from the primary to the high school standard (this is true for all types of school), there is a curious revival of it in the upper high school standards in the case of the city Afrikaans medium schools. It is as if it there receives a fresh impetus, and by the time the children are in the matriculation class the degree of adverse discrimination is more than three times as strong as in the city English medium school and more than seven times as strong as in the bilingual school. (See p. 85.)

35. Of the bilingual schools, adverse sectional discrimination is slightly greater in those where English is predominant than in those where Afrikaans is predominant. (See p. 84.)

36. Children with bilingual home environment display the least adverse discrimination. (See p. 84.)

MERE KNOWLEDGE OF THE SECOND LANGUAGE NOT ENOUGH

37. Merely learning the second language, and even reaching a fairly high proficiency in it as a subject in a unilingual school, does not necessarily imply a guarantee that with it comes a diminution of adverse sectional discrimination and a greater appreciation of, and desire to

[1] My observation in the Union Defence Force as Head of the Army Education Services and Director of Military Intelligence during the last three years "up north" and in the Union bears witness to the same increase not only in bilingualism, but also in mutual appreciation of the two sections among our soldiers, as a result of working and suffering together on a common job. The language spoken by either section was regarded as irrelevant in their association. They were simply South Africans who appreciated one another as men. (See pp. 97 *et seq.*)

co-operate with, the other section. For example, a relatively high attainment in English by children of the unilingual Afrikaans medium school in the cities was accompanied by a high degree of antagonism towards the English section. Incidentally, this high language achievement turned out to be mostly due to the contact with English which Afrikaans children in the cities get in their experience outside the school. (See p. 105.)

38. On the other hand, a poor average score in Afrikaans in unilingual English schools in the city was accompanied by a very low degree of discrimination against the Afrikaans section. If bilingualism is therefore to serve as a means of social integration something more than the study of the second language as a subject is required. Personal contact by learning, playing and living together is essential. Then children of the two sections will not only learn each other's language in the real and economical way, but, what is more important, they will also learn to understand each other. This can be done best in the bilingual school and also by a departmental scheme for the regular inter-school exchange of pupils between unilingual urban and unilingual rural areas. (See pp. 110 *et seq.*)

TEACHERS

39. A large proportion of the teachers, who have themselves come up through the unilingual school and then gone to unilingual normal or training colleges, are so lacking in understanding of the other section and are so deficient in their knowledge of the second language, that they are not fit to take charge of a class or a school where both sections are represented.

40. For example, more than half of the final year (i.e. 3rd-year post-matric.) student-teachers in the unilingual medium Transvaal normal colleges have barely a Standard VII proficiency in the second language. A considerable percentage is even below Standard VI. English and Afrikaans medium institutions are about equally poor in this respect. The situation is steadily deteriorating. (See pp. 23 *et seq.*)

41. This lack of properly trained bilingual teachers is a most serious matter, particularly for our rural children. About 60 per cent of all schools in the Union are small one- and two-teacher schools. There they have no specialist teachers for the second language, such as the larger urban schools can have. They are dependent solely on their class teacher as a model from whom to learn the second language. Actually the quality of English teaching in Afrikaans medium schools is poorer than that of Afrikaans in English medium schools, especially in the rural schools. (See p. 110.)

42. An examination of the records of the Juvenile Affairs Boards over several years shows that many of these rural boys and girls, however good their ability and character, are handicapped in their com-

petition for jobs in the cities on account of their poor knowledge of English. (See p. 106.)

43. About 40 per cent of all our children do not study further than Standard VI, and 60 per cent do not go beyond Standard VII. We cannot therefore afford to wait until the high-school stage to make them bilingual, for many never get there. (See p. 111.)

44. It is on the primary school therefore that we must concentrate if we wish to make our children bilingual. And the first and chief point of attack on this problem is the selection and training of our teachers. Here lies the crux of the whole matter. For as the teacher is, so the school will be. Radical reforms in teachers' conditions of service (e.g. salaries) as well as in training may be necessary before this problem can be solved in a long-range way. (See pp. 94 *et seq.*)

45. The teachers' attitude is of paramount importance, for it determines the emotional context in which the second language is learnt and in which children of the two sections associate with each other in the same school. (See pp. 101, 111.)

46. The following are some of the results of a survey of student-teacher attitudes in the Normal Colleges of the Transvaal:

(*a*) About three-fourths of the students felt that English and Afrikaans-speaking pupils should go to the same school and not to different schools.

(*b*) Roughly two-thirds agree that close co-operation between the two sections in South Africa is an ideal to strive for. About a quarter believe the opposite. Many hold that co-operation is futile and should not be sought. The last group was most numerous in the Afrikaans medium institutions.

(*c*) Among the students in Afrikaans medium institutions a prejudice against "racial" co-operation is accompanied by a desire to use the school for the spreading of political propaganda. This does not appear to be the case amongst English medium students. (See Chapter IX.)

THE DETERMINISTIC EFFECT OF ENVIRONMENT

47. Comparing Afrikaans home language children who attend unilingual Afrikaans medium schools (*a*) in the cities, (*b*) in the towns, (*c*) in the rural areas respectively, it was found that in their second language (English) the *town* children were nearly a year behind the *city* children, while the *rural* children were nearly a year and a half behind the *town* children.

This illustrates the deterministic effect of the environment outside the school on the child's educational achievements. It becomes, therefore, one of the major tasks of the school to compensate the child for the deficiencies of his environment. (See p. 104.) And for this task we need above all properly trained bilingual teachers. It is only when environment and school supplement each other that the school can serve as a means of social integration as well as of individual development. (See pp. 102 *et seq.*)

THE MAIN ISSUE

48. The above are some of the conclusions based on facts gathered in a survey of bilingualism which involved *inter alia* the testing of over 18,000 children and hundreds of representative schools in South Africa. According to these facts the advantages of the bilingual school over the unilingual school are clear.

49. As the regular type best adapted to meet the needs of the South African community as a whole, the bilingual school may be defined in general terms as follows: It is a type of school where English and Afrikaans-speaking children associate freely together so that they learn to know each other as well as each other's languages; and where the method of instruction is such that every child, no matter what the language of his home or of his schoolmates, is guaranteed to become an educated, bilingual South African.

50. It must however be pointed out in conclusion that, whereas the unilingual school is a device which avoids the solution of our difficulties by side-stepping them, the bilingual school is the hard way. But it is the only sure and true way in the long run.

From an organizational point of view it offers more problems than the unilingual school. To solve these will exact from the teachers and the education authorities not only much careful thought, planning and experimentation, but also a sympathetic understanding of the cultural background and aspirations of both sections. But we should not shrink from this effort if it means an ultimate benefit to the child as an individual and the building in South Africa of a united nation through the schools. The most important element in the situation is *the child*. And if it comes to the choice between his interests and administrative convenience, the child's interests must prevail.

BILINGUAL-BICULTURAL EDUCATION
IN THE UNITED STATES

An Arno Press Collection

Allen, Harold B. **A Survey of the Teaching of English to Non-English Speakers in the United States.** 1966

Allen, Virginia F. and Sidney Forman. **English As A Second Language.** [1967]

Aucamp, A.J. **Bilingual Education and Nationalism With Special Reference to South Africa.** 1926

Axelrod, Herman C. **Bilingual Background And Its Relation to Certain Aspects of Character and Personality of Elementary School Children** (Doctoral Dissertation, Yeshiva University, 1951). 1978

Bengelsdorf, Winnie. **Cthnic Studies in Higher Education.** 1972

Berrol, Selma Cantor. **Immigrants at School: New York City** (Doctoral Dissertation, City University of New York, 1967). 1978

Cordasco, Francesco, ed. **Bilingualism and the Bilingual Child.** 1978

Cordasco, Francesco, ed. **The Bilingual-Bicultural Child and the Question of   Intelligence.** 1978

Cordasco, Francesco, ed. **Bilingual Education in New York City.** 1978

Dissemination Center for Bilingual Bicultural Education. **Guide to Title VII ESEA Bilingual Bicultural Projects, 1973-1974.** 1974

Dissemination Center for Bilingual Bicultural Education. **Proceedings, National Conference on Bilingual Education.** 1975

Fishman, Joshua A. **Language Loyalty in the United States.** 1966

Flores, Solomon Hernández. **The Nature and Effectiveness of Bilingual Education Programs for the Spanish-Speaking Child in the United States** (Doctoral Dissertation, Ohio State University, 1969). 1978

Galvan, Robert Rogers. **Bilingualism As It Relates to Intelligence Test Scores and School Achievement Among Culturally Deprived Spanish-American Children** (Doctoral Dissertation, East Texas State University, 1967). 1978

Illinois State Advisory Committee. **Bilingual/Bicultural Education.** 1974

Levy, Rosemary Salomone. **An Analysis of the Effects of Language Acquisition Context Upon the Dual Language Development of Non-English Dominant Students** (Doctoral Dissertation, Columbia University, 1976). 1978

Malherbe, Ernst G. **The Bilingual School.** 1946

Mandera, Franklin Richard. **An Inquiry into the Effects of Bilingualism on Native and Non-Native Americans** (Doctoral Dissertation, University of Illinois, 1971). 1978

Materials and Human Resources for Teaching Ethnic Studies. 1975

Medina, Amelia Cirilo. **A Comparative Analysis of Evaluative Theory and Practice for the Instructional Component of Bilingual Programs** Doctoral Dissertation, Texas A&M University, 1975). 1978

National Advisory Council on Bilingual Education. **Bilingual Education.** 1975

Peebles, Robert Whitney. **Leonard Covello: A Study of an Immigrant's Contribution to New York City** (Doctoral Dissertation, New York University, 1967). 1978

Reyes, Vinicio H. **Bicultural-Bilingual Education for Latino Students** (Doctoral Dissertation, University of Massachusetts, 1975). 1978

Rodriguez M[unguia], Juan C. **Supervision of Bilingual Programs** (Doctoral Dissertation, Loyola University of Chicago, 1974). 1978

Royal Commission on Bilingualism and Biculturalism. **Preliminary Report and Books I & II.** 3 vols. in 1. 1965/1967/1968

Streiff, Paul Robert. **Development of Guidelines for Conducting Research in Bilingual Education** (Doctoral Dissertation, University of California, Los Angeles, 1974). 1978

Streiff, Virginia. **Reading Comprehension and Language Proficiency Among Eskimo Children** (Doctoral Dissertation, Ohio University, 1977). 1978

Ulibarri, Horatio. **Interpretative Studies on Bilingual Education.** 1969

United Kingdom, Department of Education and Science, National Commission for Unesco. **Bilingualism in Education.** 1965

United Nations Educational Scientific and Cultural Organization. **The Use of Vernacular Languages in Education.** 1953

United States Bureau of Indian Affairs. **Bilingual Education for American Indians.** 1971

United States Commission on Civil Rights. **Mexican American Education Study.** 5 vols. in 1. 1971-1973

United States House of Representatives. **Bilingual Education Programs.** 1967

United States House of Representatives. **United States Ethnic Heritage Studies Centers.** 1970

United States Senate. **Bilingual Education, Health, and Manpower Programs.** 1973

United States. Senate. **Bilingual Education, Hearings.** 1967

Viereck, Louis. **German Instruction in American Schools.** 1902

DATE			
NOV 8 82			
NOV 2 2 84			
DEC 14 84			
NOV 0 92			